THE RACING SAILOR'S BIBLE

THE RACING SAILOR'S BIBLE

Hervey Garrett Smith

DOUBLEDAY & COMPANY, INC., GARDEN CITY, NEW YORK

SETTING THE SPINNAKERS. (*Fusanori Nakajima.*)

Library of Congress Catalog Card Number 73–175419
Copyright © 1969, 1972 by Hervey Garrett Smith
Printed in the United States of America
First Edition

CONTENTS

THE RACING SAILOR'S BIBLE

CHAPTER 1

Conditioning and Tuning Your Boat

It has often been said that most races are won before the boat leaves the dock. All the factors relating to boat speed, boat handling, and strategy generally outweigh pure racing tactics, and the successful skipper has taken care of these problems in advance. Two thirds of the work involved in winning a race is done before the first gun is fired.

The basic element in racing is performance. From the instant you start until you cross the finish line, you must sail your boat at the maximum speed possible, and every second counts. Smoothing up a rough spot in the hull, or a slight change in the lead of a jib sheet might save only three seconds in a race that takes over two hours to complete, but those three seconds could make all the difference between winning and losing!

The first and most important requisite for successful racing is to KNOW YOUR BOAT! This doesn't mean walking around her and admiring her, or taking her out for an afternoon sail. It means *working* on her continually—hours and hours of Tender Loving Care putting and maintaining her in as near-perfect condition as possible. Only then do you achieve that kinship with your boat that all skippers aspire to. Only then do you work together as a team, with con-

fidence in yourself and your boat, and an abiding will to win. So let's get to work.

THE HULL

The first and most important step in preparing your boat for racing is to put the hull in racing condition. What you must achieve is a surface finish that is flawless—as smooth and slick as a sheet of glass. Dents, gouges, and roughness in the painted surface of the bottom increase the skin friction and drag to an amazing degree, and speed through the water is retarded correspondingly.

The procedures for getting a racing finish vary, depending on the age of the boat, her present condition, and her construction; i.e., wood or fiberglass. Since the majority of racing boats today are built of fiberglass, we'll consider them first.

If your boat is new and has never been sailed, there is not much to be done. Nevertheless, examine the hull carefully and make sure there are no dents or gouges. The marine paint manufacturers put out a variety of specially formulated products for the repair, refinishing, and maintenance of fiberglass boats. *Never* use oil-

CLOSE-HAULED TACTICS IN A STRONG WIND. (*Fusanori Nakajima.*)

base putty or surfacing compounds on a fiberglass boat—use only the polyester, two-part type.

Since all small racing craft are *dry-sailed*—that is, hauled out of the water between races—it is not necessary to use anti-fouling paint on the bottom. The epoxy enamels give the hardest, smoothest finish. Many amateurs find the epoxy enamels rather difficult to apply evenly without laps, since they set so rapidly. *Don't* use a paint roller—it gives a pebbled, textured finish that is very difficult to make smooth.

For a really perfect, mirrorlike finish, some top racing skippers take their boats to an auto body finisher to get the epoxy enamel sprayed on. He has the equipment not available to the amateur.

The factory finish on a *new* fiberglass racing boat will be, to all intents and purposes, adequate for competition. There is one thing, however, that you can do to improve it, and that is to wax the hull. Johnson's "J-Wax Kit" was especially designed for fiberglass boats. It helps preserve the gel coat and gives a high, slippery luster. Don't expect this to last all season, however. The bottom should be waxed and polished before every race.

If your boat is built of wood, perhaps molded plywood, achieving a racing finish involves more elbow grease, particularly if the boat is not new.

The best way to work is with the boat upside down, preferably under cover.

The first step is to sand off most of the paint, using aluminum oxide paper. If the boat is hard chined, with a relatively flat bottom, such as a Snipe or Lightning, an electric sander speeds up the work. Otherwise, you had best do it by hand. When you have sanded off most of the old paint and the entire surface presents a uniformly smooth appearance, dust it all off cleanly with plenty of soft rags. Be sure to get every particle of dust out of any cracks and dents that must be filled.

Next, fill those dents or imperfections with a good surfacing compound. As stated earlier, do not use the oil-base type. Remember, it may

shrink as it cures, so build it up a bit above the surface. Allow *twenty-four hours* to cure, then sand it down until the spot cannot be felt when you rub your hand over it. The hull is now ready for painting with an epoxy undercoat and a finish coat of epoxy enamel, both by the same manufacturer.

One of the peculiarities of the epoxies is that they have very poor hiding power. Therefore, the primer or undercoat should be the same color as the enamel, if possible. Apply the undercoat as evenly as you can, and then let it cure for not less than twenty-four hours. The next step is a very thorough sanding.

You'll need a bucket of warm water and a dozen or so sheets of ⚓ 4/o and ⚓ 6/o Wetor-

CLEANING THE HULL FOR MAXIMUM PERFORMANCE. (*Peter Barlow.*)

CARRY YOUR BOAT, DON'T DRAG IT. (*Peter Barlow.*)

Dry paper with a sanding block. *Do not* use an electric sander.

Put a tablespoonful of household detergent in the bucket of warm water, dip a sponge in it and wet down the whole surface. Fold a piece of ✕ 4/o over the sanding block, dip it in the water, and start sanding a small section at a time, cleaning the area with a wet sponge as you progress. The idea is to dip the paper frequently and keep the surface constantly wet. The paper is relatively inexpensive, so don't try to get a lot of mileage out of one piece.

The importance of doing a very thorough wet sanding cannot be emphasized too strongly. Paint tends to build up otherwise, and the boat becomes heavy. When you are sure the entire surface has been evenly and completely smoothed, wash it off thoroughly and give it a final going over with the finer ✕ 6/o paper. Then wash the hull carefully to remove every vestige of sanding dust and let it dry for at least half a day.

The final coat of epoxy enamel should be applied under ideal conditions . . . pick a day when it is dry and warm, and do it under cover if possible, thus avoiding direct sunlight and dust. *Read the instructions on the can* and don't use too large a brush or you'll have trouble getting an even coat.

With the hull finished, give the same attention to the centerboard and rudder—not only to the finish, but to the *shape*. If the leading and trailing edges are square or blunt, the drag or resistance is terrific. Ideally, as with airplanes, the leading edge should be rounded, and the trailing edges tapered to a knife edge. WARNING—the rules in some racing classes have restrictions governing the altering of the shape of centerboards and rudders, so read your class rules before making any changes.

Assuming the hull is now in racing condition, it is imperative that constant, meticulous care be given to *keep* it that way. The astute skipper fusses over his craft continually to insure peak performance at all times.

Right after each race the boat should be taken out of the water onto her trailer and washed off with fresh water and detergent. This is to remove every vestige of salt, slime, and dirt. If your boat has a drain plug (and it should), drain off all the water that is in the bilges. Sponge the deck, varnished trim (if any), and the interior, and clean out any sand that may have gotten in from your shoes.

To load and unload your boat from the trailer you will probably have access to a launching ramp or to a powered lift with slings maintained by most yacht clubs. Always be sure the slings and the rubber rollers on your trailer are clean and free from sand or grit. *Never* drag the boat up on the beach. If you can't use a lift or launching ramp, round up enough friends to lift the boat bodily from the water to the trailer.

While the boat is on the trailer it should be covered. If the whole boat can't be covered, it should at least have a cockpit cover to keep rainwater out. If the boat is trailered any considerable distance, you'll find that the bottom picks up road dirt, sand, and dust. These should be carefully washed off before launching, and this is a good time to give the boat a coat of wax.

SPARS AND RIGGING

Before stepping the mast and setting up the rigging, it is imperative that a minute inspection

be given every part, not only to be sure that the entire rig is in working order, but to detect flaws that could lead to breakdowns. A missing cotter pin in a turnbuckle, a loose tang on the mast, or a single broken strand in a wire shroud could, if undetected, lead to a dismasting.

Go over every inch of the wire shrouds and stays and look for broken strands. Examine minutely the terminal fittings, whether they be swaged-on sockets or nicropress sleeves. Look for minute cracks or corrosion that would indicate metal fatigue, and if the condition of the metal looks suspicious, see that the part is replaced immediately. It is better to be safe than sorry!

Wooden spars require constant attention. Tangs, sail track, and other fittings are generally secured by wood screws or through bolts. With the alternate expansion and contraction of the wood over a period of time, the fastenings have a habit of working loose, particularly wood screws. Check each one . . . and you'll find you can take up half a turn or more on many of them. The main halyard sheave is generally hung on a through bolt. Put a wrench on the nut and see if it is set up properly.

At the start of the racing season the masthead sheave should be removed and the through bolt or pin should be generously greased with Lubriplate, the lubricant used in outboard motors.

The sail track on the mast and boom is subject to a certain amount of corrosion. Judicious use of fine emery paper followed by wiping with an oily rag will clean it and prevent sail slides from sticking. But if you have grooved spars instead of sail track, rub a piece of paraffin up and down the slot or groove to make the bolt rope of your sail slide freely.

Every turnbuckle should be opened up and the threads liberally greased with Lubriplate. See that they are fitted with *new* cotter pins of the correct size!

A can of heavy-body or electric motor oil (SAE-20) should be your constant companion, not only during tune-up time, but throughout the racing season. There are few mechanical

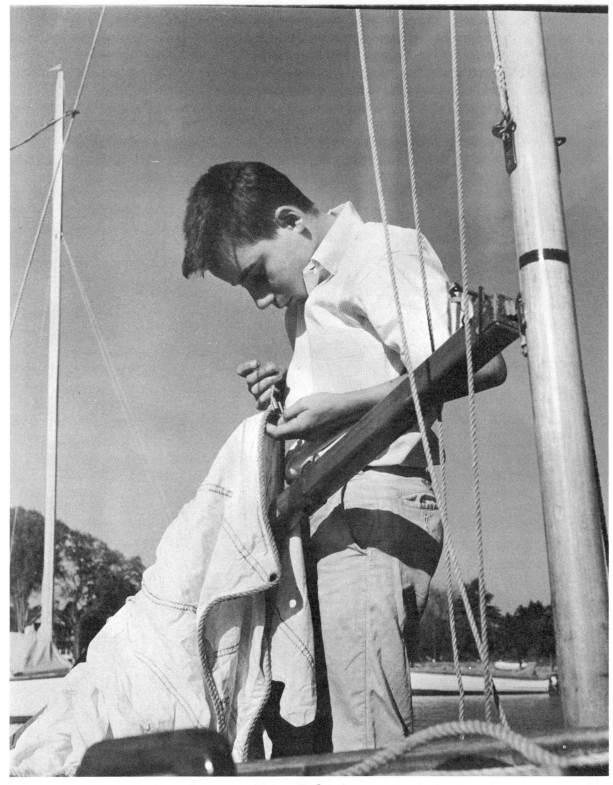

CHECKING THE CONDITION OF THE SAILS. (*Peter Barlow.*)

parts that will not work better when oiled. A snap shackle that won't open quickly, a block sheave that won't turn freely, or a cam cleat that sticks . . . each can cause the loss of those precious seconds that win or lose races.

Before every race, oil or grease every block and fitting that has movable parts. And be sure to wipe off any excess with a clean rag. Winches should be completely dismantled and greased with Lubriplate.

All running rigging should be overhauled and checked for wear, and see that all rope ends are properly whipped. If a rope is badly frayed and ratty looking, replace it with new rope. In my opinion, the finest rope for running rigging is Samson's Yacht Braid. The outer cover is dacron, and the core is polypropylene. It has minimum stretch and maximum strength. Compared to common laid rope, it will last longer and run through blocks more freely and with less friction, and it is less liable to kink or foul. Cam cleats tend to chew up and abrade a laid rope, but Yacht Braid seems to resist this tendency.

SAILS

Since sails are the motive power that drives your boat you want the best obtainable. While some of the more affluent skippers have two or four suits of sails designed for various weather conditions, most of us are forced to take the sails that came with the boat and do the best with what we have. The sailmaker has probably done the best he could, and the rest is up to you.

If your sails have too much or too little draft, don't be discouraged . . . this can be corrected to a large extent by varying the tension on the luff and foot.

Unless the sails are new, you should inspect them carefully, on both sides, to see if any of the stitching is frayed or broken. In the old days when sails were made of cotton, the stitching would sink into the surface of the cloth. But with the modern synthetics, the stitching lies on the surface and, therefore, is not protected against chafe and wear. It is often said that "sails don't wear out, but the stitching does." When this occurs the sails should be sent back to the maker for resewing.

There is one point that should be emphasized —KEEP YOUR SAILS CLEAN. You should wash them periodically, mainly to remove all traces of salt. The best way is to immerse them in a large tub of cold water. If they are dirty as well as salty, add a little liquid Lux to the water. If you don't have a tub large enough, drape them smoothly over a clothes line and use a garden hose. Do it on a day when there is little wind, and leave them hanging till dry. DON'T cram them in the sail bag—fold them neatly.

Sail battens may seem rather insignificant items to be concerned with, but they have an important bearing on performance. All too often they are too heavy, too stiff, or too long. Battens are generally made of ash, and they should be tapered . . . thinner toward the inner end. Be sure they are sanded very smooth and rounded at the end so that they don't chafe the sailcloth. Check the length . . . they should be at least a half-inch shorter than the batten pocket.

Several firms are making battens of plastic or fiberglass. In my opinion they are better than wood battens because they are much lighter in weight and more flexible.

One final note on caring for your sails. All synthetics have a rather low melting point. This means that the greatest enemy is chafe and friction. NEVER leave a sail hoisted when the boat is lying at a dock or mooring. Slatting and flogging back and forth in a breeze cause excessive chafe and wear in cloth and stitching, can ruin the shape of the sail, and definitely shorten the sail's useful life.

REQUIRED OR NECESSARY EQUIPMENT

In the small one-design racing boats, class rules specify the minimum allowable weight of the boat, and if you hope to win you'll be sure your boat comes as close to that minimum as possible. Personal gear and unnecessary equipment are so much dead weight and contribute nothing to the speed of the boat—they just go along for the ride. It is surprising how much unnecessary junk accumulates aboard a boat. In the larger racing-cruising auxiliaries weight is not a critical factor, and there is ample stowage space. But in the small boat, if it is unnecessary, leave it ashore!

LIFE PRESERVERS

There are a number of U. S. Coast Guard-approved life preservers available that are excellent, in that they will float a person face up, even though he be unconscious and/or a non-

ELVSTRÖM LIFE JACKET. (*Canor Plarex, Inc.*)

swimmer. But for the small-boat racing sailor they are totally unsuitable since they are too bulky for wearing continually, greatly restrict freedom of movement, and are decidedly uncomfortable.

Common sense dictates that the skipper and crew *wear* life preservers at all times when afloat. The vest-type preservers are the best. Flat, close-fitting, and very light in weight, they do not impede even the most violent body action. In fact, you hardly know you are wearing one.

The Elvström life jacket and the Sans Souci life vest are excellent examples of this type. Both have pockets, and are so compact they can be worn under a sweater or rain gear. The flotation material is closed-cell foam.

A preserver of different construction, the Flotherchoc, is light as a feather. Flotation consists of numerous hermetically sealed plastic cells or tubes sewn into the nylon vest. This is the lightest of all jackets, and the one most favored by youngsters.

One important note: Boat cushions are NOT life preservers!

PUMPS AND BAILERS

Racing is a wet sport, and water is bound to come aboard in varying degrees—in little dollops of spray or in buckets of solid water. There must be some means of getting it out, *during* as well as after the race. Many racing boats, particularly the fiberglass ones, have self-bailing cockpits, which obviate the need for a pump.

Most of the high-performance, planing boats, such as the Flying Dutchman and Tempest, are fitted with suction bailers. Basically, a suction bailer is a trap door that when opened lets the water flow out. It can be used *only* on a reach or a run, and it begins to work when the boat speed reaches about 5 or 6 mph. It is fitted with a flap that acts as a check valve to keep the water from spouting back in when the boat slows down. Two bailers are required, one in

SANS SOUCI LIFE VEST. (*Ship Shop, Inc.*)

each bilge. The suction bailer has a wire locking arm that prevents accidental opening and pulls the trap flush and tight.

All boats that are trailered should be fitted with transom bailers, not only to take care of rain water, but to facilitate draining when the boat is hauled out.

While there are some skippers who are so weight-conscious that they wouldn't think of carrying a bilge pump, you'd be wise to have one aboard. There are some very efficient and very light-weight all-plastic pumps available that are easy to use and easy to stow. Four to six strokes will remove a gallon of water. A Du Pont cellulose sponge is a must. It can be used as a bailer to remove small pockets of water that are trapped and to clean the boat after the race. Keep it aboard at all times.

ANCHORS

An anchor might be classed as a necessary evil—it must be heavy enough to hold your boat,

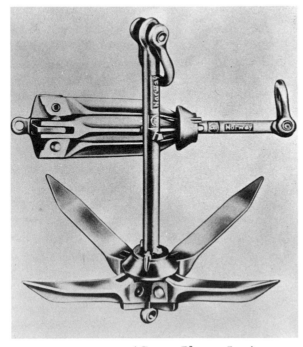

A FOLDING ANCHOR. (*Canor Plarex, Inc.*)

and it is awkward to stow. You can't do anything to cut down its weight, but you can simplify the stowage problem.

The trouble with most anchors is that the flukes and stock seem to snag on everything even though, as with the Danforth type, they lie perfectly flat. But there is an anchor that is non-fouling and easy to stow. The SAV folding anchor has four flukes, arranged radially like a grapnel. They fold up along the shank and are held in the closed position by a ring or collar, which slides down and locks the flukes in the open position. Thus, the anchor when folded is, in effect, a smooth cylinder shape with nothing protruding to catch on a sheet or line.

Your anchor line should be nylon, and quarter-inch diameter is adequate for small craft up to about 22 feet overall. As to length, it depends on the depth of water. It should be long enough to allow a scope of 6 to 1; that is, 60 feet if the depth is 10 feet.

STOP WATCH

While stop watches are made for all sports, the true yachting timer differs in that it shows the *time left*, rather than elapsed time. The best ones have a five-minute repeating hand. The most expensive ones are waterproof and are recommended if you can afford them. Some are worn on the wrist, but most skippers prefer one that is hung on a lanyard around the neck. When not in use it can be dropped inside your shirt.

Since precise, accurate timing is all-important, I advise you to get the best that you can afford.

COMPASS

Every boat, no matter how small, should have a compass aboard, even if it is only a Boy Scout pocket compass. A small racing compass with 45-degree lubber lines enables you to plot wind shifts and tactical courses.

On boats with ample side decks the compass can be flush-mounted on the deck near the forward end of the cockpit, where it may be read by both skipper and crew. Some boats, notably those in the Star class, mount two this way, one on each deck. Others mount the compass just under the deck at the forward end of the cockpit, on the floor just aft of the centerboard trunk, or on the trunk itself. Wherever you carry it, a compass can help you win races!

MASTHEAD FLY

As a constant, accurate indicator of the direction of the *apparent* wind, a masthead fly is indispensable. Your sails must be trimmed in relation to it at all times. If a competitor is up to windward of you, a glance at the fly will tell you if you are in his wind shadow. Every wind shift will be instantly revealed by the fly.

The fly is permanently fixed to the masthead. It should be small, extremely light, properly balanced so that it is not affected by heeling, and offer the least amount of wind resistance or drag. So choose your type according to these specifications.

TELLTALES

Supplementary to the masthead fly, telltales are equally necessary. There are various patented telltales of plastic or metal, which are balanced and which clip to the shrouds. But the common do-it-yourself variety are simply short lengths of colored knitting wool, say ten or twelve inches long, tied on each shroud about five feet off the deck.

They are so light and sensitive they will fly in the faintest zephyr. They are not as true an indication of the apparent wind as the masthead fly, since they are subject to influence of deflection from the sails, but they are always in your line of sight. Without them you'd soon get a stiff neck from constantly lifting your head to look aloft.

The slightest variation in wind direction is instantly revealed, telling you to luff or bear away. But it takes practice—hours of sailing by the telltales—to develop an automatic response to their indications.

PROTEST FLAG

The N.A.Y.R.U. racing rules require the *prompt* hoisting of a protest flag, the square red code flag "B" when an alleged foul has been committed, and kept flying until you finish the race. And by prompt, they mean *right away*, not fifteen minutes or half an hour later. It doesn't require that you have an actual code flag aboard—any piece of red cloth (except the ensign) hung where it is visible will do. Tie it to a shroud or on the boom, immediately after you believe an infringement has occurred.

EMERGENCY

No matter how careful you may be, there is always the possibility of a breakdown—a spectacular accidental jibe, a collision with a competitor's boat, or a rigging failure can result in a situation requiring immediate emergency repairs.

A cruising auxiliary will carry a complete tool kit, with spare parts, fastenings, and assorted hardware. But this is impractical on the small racing boat, where stowage space is limited and the extra weight is detrimental. However, there are a few items that should be carried that weigh very little and require very little space.

A small coil of quarter-inch dacron line can serve in many ways—as a spare sheet, for one—and it will weigh but a few ounces. I recommend a small ditty bag (which can be tucked anywhere) containing the following: a roll of contact-adhesive dacron tape for emergency sail repairs, a little can of oil, a small screw driver, a pair of pliers, a couple of shackles, a small ball of waxed nylon twine for seizings, and if you have a spinnaker, a roll of Rip-Stop spinnaker mending tape.

Ever since a horrendous night many years ago, when only the fact that I was wearing a sheath knife at my belt saved my boat and my life, I have never gone sailing without a knife on my person. A sheath knife combination set, worn at the belt, has a marlinspike and combination shackle opener—screw driver and pliers. Of course, if your boat is one of the high-performance jobs requiring frequent acrobatics by skipper and crew, a sheath knife could conceivably be a hindrance. In that case a stainless steel rigging knife would be preferable. It has a folding blade and self-locking marlinspike and is secured with a lanyard and tucked in your pocket.

The foregoing items I consider to be basic essentials, suitable for the smallest classes. As the size of your boat steps up, you can add to them as your experience and judgment dictate.

TUNING UP

Assuming the boat and its gear are now in racing condition, the next step is to rig up. This should be done with the boat in the water, preferably on a calm day, or at least in a sheltered spot where it is quiet.

With the mast stepped and the standing rigging hooked up, the first step is to determine if the mast is plumb athwartship, leaning neither to port nor starboard. There are several ways to do this. You can haul the end of a steel tape to the masthead on the halyard and measure carefully to a point on one chain plate, then to a corresponding point on the other side. On larger craft, *providing* the boat is absolutely level athwartship, a plumb bob or weight hung on the halyard will reveal if the masthead is off-center.

Explicit instructions for setting up the rigging cannot be given here since they differ with the many classes of boats. Methods of staying the mast will vary from the simple two-shrouds-and-a-jibstay, to the complex rigs employing two or three sets of shrouds, jumper stays, runners, adjustable backstays and others, so the best we can do is to cover the basic factors. Even the experts admit it is primarily a matter of trial and error.

Rake: All boats seem to work better with a little rake to the mast. In a cat-rigged boat, such as the Penguin, the mast should rake aft more than one that is sloop-rigged, and at *no* time should it be raked forward. Unless you are sure what is normal for your type of boat, do a little detective work and see how your competitors do it.

Tension: No standing rigging should be set up so tight you can play a tune on it, or so loose you can tie knots in it! Shrouds should be just tight enough to prevent the mast's leaning to one side or the other when the boat is under sail. If the boat has two sets of shrouds, the lower shroud should have a little less tension than the upper. The only way to check for proper tensions is to sight up the sail track when *under sail*. It should appear straight from deck to masthead, or have a very slight, fair curve to *leeward* on both tacks.

The jibstay must be taut at all times to keep the luff of the jib straight without sagging to leeward. A sagging jibstay is an abomination. It spoils the designed shape of the sail, makes it baggy, and backwinds the mainsail. The stronger the wind, the more the jib sags, and this is disastrous when close-hauled.

If the boat has jumper stays, they should be set up just enough to bend the masthead forward *slightly* when the boat is at rest. Then, when the jib is set up and you are under way, the tension on the luff will straighten the mast.

When the rigging has been set up to your satisfaction, put the cotter pins in every turnbuckle. One missing cotter pin could lead to dismasting. Then tape each turnbuckle smoothly. Seaboard's Sea Tape is excellent for the purpose. It is waterproof, and it can also be used as a temporary substitute for whippings on rope ends.

With the standing rigging properly set, the

RIGGING UP. (*Peter Barlow.*)

next step is to check the running rigging, and we begin with the jib.

The performance of the jib is critically affected by the lead of the jib sheets—how far out from the centerline of the boat, and how far aft. The athwartship location of the jib sheet block can be plotted easily. For the average racing boat it should be on the 10½-degree line. Measure aft from the point of attachment of the jibstay along the centerline of the boat, and at exactly five feet put a mark on the deck. Now measure out on each side of the centerline from the mark, and at right angles, exactly 11⅛ inches and place a mark at each point.

CENTERLINE

10½°   10½°

the wind as possible, then start to luff gradually. If the jib breaks or luffs first in the upper part, near the head, the lead is too far aft, and if it breaks first near the tack, it is too far forward. If the lead is correctly placed, the jib should break evenly from head to tack.

Before getting any deeper into the subject of tuning, you should make a careful study of the rules of your class. All one-design-class rules contain certain restrictions, designed to keep all the boats as nearly alike as possible. They govern such matters as weights and measurements of hulls, spars, and sails, and their limits of tolerances and proscribed alterations.

As an example, it is generally agreed that for optimum performance a main-sheet traveler is almost indispensable. But take note that in a few classes, the Lightning class for an example, main-sheet travelers are not allowed.

Therefore, *know your class rules,* for if you make any changes in your boat that do not conform, you are subject to disqualification.

In any one-design class it has been determined that the differences in boat speeds are primarily due to maladjusted sails. A perfectly cut mainsail can perform badly if it is not set properly, and conversely, the shape of a poor sail can be improved greatly by proper handling.

You can control the shape of a mainsail, or alter it to suit different wind conditions, by changing the tension or amount of stretch on the luff and foot and, where permitted, by altering the curvature of the sail by flexing the mast or boom.

Setting up on the downhaul to increase tension on the luff will move the maximum draft of the sail forward, flatten the sail, and ease the leach. Tightening the outhaul will likewise flatten the sail and pull the draft down nearer the boom. You strive to make your mainsail full for light air and flat for beating to windward in heavy breezes.

Bending the mast to remove draft when going to windward is a very effective way of increasing boat speed. Some boats have a highly

Now, a line from the jibstay passing through each of these marks will form an angle of 10½ degrees with the centerline. Somewhere along each line is the point to which the jib sheet should be trimmed. On most boats there is a length of track installed on this line, so that the jib sheet can be moved forward or aft.

The fore and aft position can be determined only by trial and error under sail. This will vary with the cut of the jib. Sail the boat as close to engineered and sophisticated rig, such as the mast on a Star boat. On a Star, bending is accomplished with jumper struts and adjustable lower backstays, and by moving the mast forward or aft at the deck.

On boats having only a simple three-wire rig, such as the Snipe and Penguin, limited bending is accomplished by planing down the mast to get the maximum flexibility. If your boat has aluminum spars, you can forget the "bendy" rig.

Tuning your boat cannot be done in a day. It requires hours and days of sailing and observing. I am reminded of the story of a young man walking up Fifth Avenue, in New York, with a violin case under his arm, who stopped an old man and asked, "Can you tell me how to get to Carnegie Hall?" And the old man replied, "Practice, my boy, practice!"

You and your crew must get out and practice every available moment, alert and observant. Sailing as close-hauled as possible, experiment with the trim of the jib. When you have the point where you achieve the maximum speed, note the position of the jib sheet and mark it. By that I mean place a mark on each jib sheet where it enters the deck block. A felt-tip pen, a crayon, or even a lipstick will leave a permanent mark.

Then, each time you come about, your crew *trims to the mark*. He has an instant reference point that can be seen at a glance, and precious seconds are not lost playing with the sheet.

Experiment with varying the tension on the downhaul and clew outhaul on the mainsail, on a day when the wind is moderate or "average" for the locality. When you feel the boat has achieved optimum speed, put a mark on the boom and mast to indicate the exact position of the outhaul fitting and the gooseneck fitting. Thus in a heavy wind you stretch the foot and luff of the sail a little *beyond* the marks, and in light airs a little short of the marks.

Improper trimming of the main sheet when going to windward can noticeably reduce the speed of the boat. The position of the sheet block on the traveler is a very critical one. If it is too far inboard, particularly on a reach, you'll be trimming *in* rather than *down,* and the leach of the sail will have an undesirable twist. Overtrimming causes a tight leach, and the sail does not have the proper angle with the wind; the use of more rudder is required, and excessive drag is set up.

In light winds, where the main objective is to obtain the maximum driving force, the boom should be trimmed well amidship when close-hauled, and as the wind increases, the mainsheet traveler should be eased out.

It should be noted that the genoa jib is the primary driving sail, and its efficiency is much greater than that of the mainsail. To put it another way, it has a greater driving force per square foot of the sail area than the main. It guides the air flow on to the mainsail in the area adjacent to the mast, and the most efficient flow through the slot is obtained when the overlapped portion of the genoa is approximately parallel to the adjacent part of the main. Therefore, the shape of the leech of a genoa is of critical importance. Any tendency of the leech to curve inward is very detrimental, as it disturbs the free flow of air through the slot and absorbs useful energy. This is a common fault of many genoas, and a cause of concern to all racing skippers. Happy is he who has a jib with a perfectly set leech.

With your boat sailing to windward as close as possible, observe the leech in different wind forces. If it curves inward, try moving the jib sheet lead a bit aft. Sometimes this will ease the leach enough to correct it. If not, you had best send the sail back to the sailmaker for recutting.

Another detrimental factor overlooked by many skippers is the gap between the foot of the genoa and the deck. It should be reduced as much as possible. So be sure the tack of the genoa is as close to the deck as the fittings will allow.

CHAPTER 2

Your Crew

A really first-class crew is worth his weight in gold, and how he performs depends on you, the skipper. As a team you and he must be able to work together in close harmony, and you should be willing to devote all the time and effort required toward obtaining and training the best possible crew.

What qualities should you look for in selecting a crew? He should have a high I.Q., a keen sense of competition, and mental and physical agility. Needless to say, his personality should be compatible with your own.

Above all, a good crew must be dependable. There's nothing more frustrating than having to search frantically for a substitute an hour before race time because your regular crew failed to show up. You want someone who will stick with you race after race, who wants to win as much as you do, and who takes his responsibilities seriously.

Try to get a crew who has had as much sailing experience as you, and if he has had racing experience, all the better. To be sure, a greenhorn can be trained, but it would take too much time and most certainly take away some of your self-confidence.

Teamwork is the absolute essential, and a win-

ning skipper-crew combination can be achieved only by hours and hours of sailing together. Furthermore, the spirit of "togetherness" is needed ashore as well as afloat. Your crew should be willing and anxious to help in the pre-season overhaul and maintenance, for only then does he get to know your boat as well as you, and become fully aware that he is an integral part of the team. Many skippers complain about crew members who get all steamed up about a race but are never around when work is to be done.

The crew who will be racing with you should also be with you in tuning up, for two reasons. First, he gets proficient in sail handling, learns the boat's peculiarities, and develops instant reflexes, so that he automatically reacts to sudden changes in wind direction by trimming sheets for maximum speed, with no lost motion.

Secondly, and more important, he gets to know *you*, the skipper. He observes how your mind works, how you react in various situations, what you expect of him. He learns to do his job intuitively, without orders from you. These are the things that lead to perfect harmony and teamwork.

There is another thing you can do to increase efficiency—let your crew take the helm once in a

WORKING TOGETHER IN HARMONY. (*Peter Barlow.*)

while. Some skippers fail to recognize how important this is. In tuning up and in pre-race trials your crew should be given ample opportunity to try his hand at skippering. He gets to know the feel of the boat, and the whole picture takes on a new aspect. He'll have a better appreciation of the skipper's problems, and crewing becomes more meaningful.

In actual racing, I occasionally let my crew spell me on the downwind leg. I do not advise it on the beat to windward, because no one can work the boat upwind as well as the skipper.

For your crew, there are two types of individuals you should avoid like the plague. First there's the know-it-all, the argumentative smart-aleck who thinks he knows more than you do and makes a point of letting you know it. He criticizes every move you make, and responds to every order with an objection. You cannot teach him anything because he doesn't want to learn. There can be only one skipper, and that is you. You are the one to make the decisions, right or wrong, and you must sail your own race.

Then there's the chatterbox, whose incessant yackety drives you to distraction. There is no room for conversation when you are racing. All your senses must be concentrated on the job at hand, every moment. That goes for your crew, too. Unnecessary talk impairs your efficiency, disrupts your thinking, and thereby gives your competitors an edge.

As I have stated earlier, the skipper is responsible for the performance of the crew. Treat him like a human being, and remember you are not the captain of a slave ship. If he pulls a boner, don't cuss him out—you'll probably make just as many mistakes as he. When he does a particularly smart piece of sail handling, compliment him sincerely. He likes to know his work is appreciated.

You should practice jibing and tacking, over and over, until the procedure becomes smooth and automatic. Your crew should act intuitively, without any order from you, and with a minimum of movement. Every time you or your crew shifts position, the boat's speed is reduced.

In the light displacement centerboard boats the placement of live ballast (you and your crew) is very important. It should be concentrated amidships, or near the center of balance of the boat. So sit fairly close together and keep away from the ends of the boat. At times, particularly when you are handling a spinnaker, it is necessary for your crew to be forward, but he should be made to understand that every second he is away from his normal sailing position the boat's speed is being killed. Those hurtful seconds can be reduced only by practice and training.

One vitally important duty of your crew is handling the stop watch and timing the starts. Starts demand intense concentration by the skipper, and accurate, precise timing. The preferred method of calling the time is as follows:

Your crew starts his watch at the warning gun. He first calls out the minutes to go— "9-8-7-6-5-"—and then calls the half-minutes —"4½-4-3½-3-2½-2-1½-1." At this point he calls the five-second intervals—"55-50-45-" etc. At 30 seconds he calls "down shape!" and you know you have 30 seconds left before the preparatory gun. He then starts calling off the last thirty seconds, ending with "-4-3-2-1-GUN!"

Impress upon your crew that only the *shape* (flag, cone, ball, or cylinder) marks the *official* time—*not* the puff of smoke or the sound of the cannon. Guns often misfire, and the gunner may be slow on the trigger.

In addition to the crew's stop watch, you'll need to be wearing a wrist watch, for this reason. Let us assume that there are six classes in the race. You have consulted the race circular and noted that your class starts at 2 P.M., and the class before yours starts at 1:50. Unless your watch is synchronized with that of the official timer on the committee boat, you will not know when to *expect* the gun. Your watch may show the correct time, but when the previous class starts, you can be sure that as far as the committee is concerned, it is 1:50, even though your watch reads 1:35! Failure to synchronize your watch can ruin a start for fair.

There's one other use for the stop watch besides timing your start, and that is for tuning up. When you practice tacking, determine how long it takes to come about, in various degrees of wind. Time yourself from the moment you start to luff to the moment you fill away on the other tack. Knowing exactly how many seconds it takes is extremely important in timing your starts. Having learned your tacking time when you are beating to windward, time yourself for a 180-degree tack on a beam reach—in other words, for doubling back on your course with the wind abeam.

"I am the Captain, and my word is law!" This attitude might have been acceptable in the days of Captain Bligh, but it has no place in a racing boat. Your crew should share in all your plans and problems. If you want something done in a certain way, explain to him *why* you insist on it. Pre-race plans and strategy, analysis of weather conditions, and race tactics should be frankly discussed with him, and he should be encouraged to express his opinions. They may differ from yours, but you make the final decisions, according to your judgment, and if you are mistaken, be fair enough to admit it.

After a particularly bad performance it is all too easy to blame your crew or the boat when the actual fault lies with you, the skipper. If your crew was very inept, it is because you didn't train him properly. If your boat was not properly tuned, *you* are responsible for lack of foresight, not your crew.

In the final analysis, a skipper and crew must be objective if they want to win. Perfect co-ordination of thought and action can be achieved only when they have mutual confidence and respect.

CHAPTER 3

Weather, Tide, and Wind

If you hope to be a consistent winner, you'll need a better-than-average understanding of these three vitally important factors. Your pre-race planning of tactics and strategy must be based on your ability to foretell with reasonable accuracy what the weather will be doing in your locality during the entire race.

Armed with this knowledge, as an astute skipper you will anticipate wind shifts, make tidal currents work for you not against you, and set the draft of your sails according to the expected wind strength.

It is not necessary for you to become a meteorologist, but it *is* possible for you to become proficient in local short-range weather forecasting. All it takes is an understanding of the basic principles that govern the weather and an observant eye to read the signs that are all about you. Day-by-day studies of weather patterns in your particular area, supplemented by weather maps, regional forecasts, and the barometer, are the means by which you acquire what is called "local knowledge."

I earnestly recommend *Eric Sloane's Weather Book* for a non-technical explanation of meteorology and weather forecasting. It will help you to understand the meaning of high- and low-pressure patterns, warm and cold fronts, barometric pressure, and the movement of winds.

The weather map that you find in your daily paper gives a graphic picture of the prevailing weather throughout the nation on a particular day, and is an invaluable aid in forecasting. However, it should be remembered that weather moves east across the country, because of the rotation of the earth, and the map is about twelve hours old when you receive your paper. This means that the cold front shown over your area has already moved five hundred miles to the east. Therefore, to determine what the weather will probably be on race day, study the weather map of the day *before* the race and learn to look to the *west* for changes.

You should own a good barometer, and if you expect to be weather-wise, you'll consult it at least twice a day. While the weather map reveals conditions in a general area, the barometer pin points conditions right in your own front yard, and within a shorter range.

Your barometer may bear the words *stormy, fair, changeable*. Ignore them. What we are interested in is not the barometric pressure at a single reading, but its tendency—whether it is

APPROACHING SQUALL. (*Peter Barlow.*)

rising or falling, and how fast. Tap the barometer; if the hand moves to the right the barometer is rising; if to the left, it is falling. If the hand takes a *big jump* when you tap it, it is telling you that the pressure is rising or falling *rapidly*, and you can expect a change of weather in a matter of an hour or two, generally accompanied by much stronger winds.

A low barometer is usually associated with bad weather—rain and strong winds—and a high barometer is accompanied by fair skies and low humidity. If race day comes when you have been having a spell of fair weather and the barometer has been *stationary*, you can expect moderate to light winds with no appreciable change during the race.

A friend of mine who once lived on the east end of Long Island bought a new barometer—a very expensive one. When it arrived he hung it on the wall and retired for the night. When he arose at dawn he was horrified to see the hand was at the bottom of the dial—indicating *hurricane*. Now, a hurricane was unthinkable on Long Island, and believing that he had been sold a faulty instrument, he hopped in his car and headed for New York where he had bought it.

Well, he never got there, and when he returned home, there *was* no home—it was utterly obliterated in the hurricane of 1938!

Barometers never lie, and you had better believe it. Get in the habit of checking your barometer the first thing in the morning and the last thing at night, and as often in between as possible. It is one infallible tool you can rely on if you can properly interpret its message.

I consider a radio an absolute necessity as an aid in short-range forecasting; specifically, I recommend a small marine portable with three bands—beacon, marine, and broadcast. On the 190–400 KC Beacon band you can get up-to-the-minute, accurate forecasts from FAA weather navigation stations. They give wind speed and direction, barometric pressure, precipitation, and visibility. Most important, they give flash warnings of dangerous weather—line squalls and thunderstorms.

The marine weather-navigation stations are found in the 1.6–4.5 MC Marine-band frequencies. They provide area weather, wind, tide and sea conditions, and forecasts of high winds, fog, and rain.

On the broadcast band, your local radio station will occasionally interrupt its rock-and-roll program for its version of "weather." This I can do without—a glance out of the window will be more revealing and more accurate.

Weather broadcasts from the nearest airport are the most timely, and most useful to the racing sailor in that they foretell the wind for the *next two hours*. And so, when race day arrives, get the airport weather at the last possible moment before starting time.

TIDE

Tidal currents must be considered of prime concern when you race in coastal waters. If you are a wise skipper, you know in advance what the direction and force of the current will be during the race, and you will use that knowledge in planning your strategy, striving to turn it to your advantage.

On the long beat to windward you must know the direction of the current in relation to the wind direction, and you take the tack that brings the current against the lee bow. Lee-

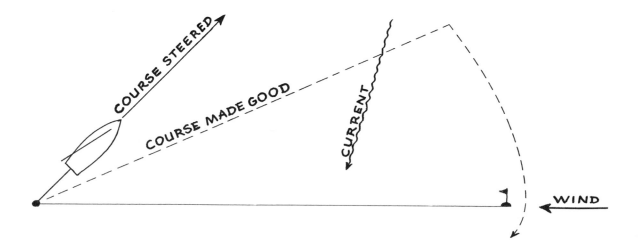

bowing the current has the effect of moving your boat to windward over the bottom, toward the mark. Conversely, the current against your weather bow pushes you away from the mark, to leeward.

When you are beating to windward against a strong current whose direction is such that you cannot get a lee bow on either tack, take the tack that brings you nearer the shore, for there is where the current is weaker.

On a reach or run, don't head directly for the

velocity is attained approximately three hours after, on each tide.

Also helpful are the Tidal Current Charts, also prepared by the Coast and Geodetic Survey. These charts for any given area show by means of arrows and figures the *hourly* direction and velocities of the tidal currents. While they may not give precise data for your particular race course, because of their small scale, they do give a general picture of current movements in your area.

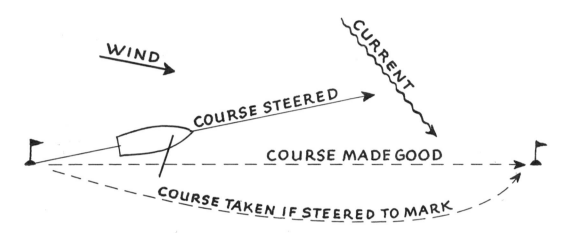

next mark unless the current runs parallel to that leg. With the current running across the course, heading for the mark will result in sailing a greater distance over the bottom, and your track will describe an arc, rather than a straight line.

To acquire information on currents, you need two publications—the *Tide Tables* and the *Current Tables*, published yearly by the U. S. Coast and Geodetic Survey. The *Tide Tables* give you the times of high and low water in your locality for every day in the year. The *Current Tables* give you the times of slack water before flood and before ebb, the times of maximum flood and ebb, and the velocity of this maximum current in each case.

Slack water is that period during the turn of the tides when the velocity of the current is slight or barely discernible. Maximum current

All these published data must be supplemented by our old friend "local knowledge." The signs are all about you. Channel buoys lean over with the current and the water swirls around them. An anchored boat lies at an angle to the wind as the current shoves her sideways. When a channel buoy is on the edge of a clearly defined shoal or flat, you will note that it leans over farther than the other buoys, indicating greater current velocity. Where a point of land extends far out into tidewater, you'll note increased velocity as the current is funneled through.

Study your navigational chart and draw your race course on it. Notice the depth of water all around the course, the configuration of the adjacent shoreline, and any ledges or shoals near the course. All these things have an influence on the force and direction of tidal currents,

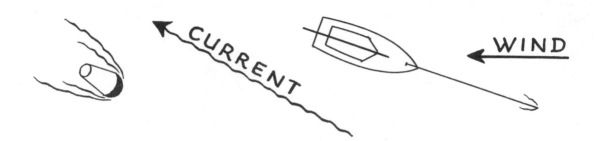

and they should be firmly fixed in your mind.

Tides have a direct relationship with the wind. At the time of slack water when flood begins, you can expect a noticeable increase in the force of the wind. In places where strong tide rips occur, winds will be strong during maximum current velocity.

WIND

Although wind is a part of predictable weather, its character will vary with different localities. Day-by-day observation over a long period will reveal that it follows a fairly consistent pattern in your area. Local winds are affected by geographical variations, such as flatland areas, hills and valleys, and bays or indentations along the shoreline.

Temperature variations play a big part in the actions of the winds. On a nice summer day, the wind coming in from the sea flows over water which has a constantly cool temperature.

The breeze will be steady and true. When it hits the heated land it will fluctuate in varying degrees, but by then it is no longer of particular concern to the sailor.

A breeze blowing *from* the land, however, is a different matter. Hot, dry air rises in strong vertical currents over the land, and when it meets the cooler, moist air over the water, a marked turbulence occurs. Thus, the northwesters of the eastern seaboard are gusty and very shifty. This is most pronounced close to the shore, and the wind becomes steadier as it moves farther out to sea.

The northwester is the least desirable wind for racing because of its great fluctuations in strength and direction. Sailing the windward leg in a northwester, therefore, requires special strategy, and you must be extremely alert for wind shifts.

Always bear in mind that the nearer you get to land, the more the wind *off* the land tends to blow *at right angles to the shoreline*, and the more gusty it becomes. But above all else, you

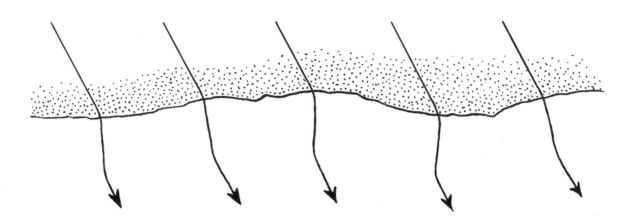

must learn to capitalize on the continual wind shifts of a northwester. The basic principle is to *tack on the headers*. In a steady and true southwest wind you make as few tacks as possible. But in a northwester the reverse is true. The minute you are headed, *tack!* Don't bear off and wait for the header to pass. Don't worry too much about covering your competitor—pay more attention to the wind shifts and you are more liable to come out on top.

Down on the Great South Bay, on the south shore of Long Island, where I live, a northwester seldom lasts more than a day and a half. Then it fades away and in comes our well-known southwester, strong and steady! We know that this welcome wind shift always comes exactly at the turn of the tide as it starts to flood. We can smell it coming, and can generally predict its arrival within fifteen minutes.

On a hot summer day there is a 50–50 chance of thunderstorms or squalls. A mass of black, turbulent clouds with sharply defined edges suddenly builds up in the west and you know that within a very short time you'll be hit with violent wind and rain. These sudden storms can be vicious and should be treated with caution and respect.

If a squall comes up during a race, you are faced with the problem of whether to drop out or continue, and the decision must be made quickly. It can be a tough question. Squalls are invariably of very short duration, but they can be light and harmless or violent and dangerous. You must decide on the basis of your experience and self-confidence.

If you have any doubts, drop your sails and anchor! With the passing of the worst part of the squall you may find you are still very much in the race. If, on the other hand, you feel you can safely weather the blow, *head over toward the squall.* Now this may not sound right, but you must remember that the *new* wind will be coming from those black clouds toward you. Thus you will have the weather berth over your less-observant competitors! The outcome of many races has been decided during a squall.

CHAPTER 4

Helmsmanship

Cornelius Shields, one of the foremost authorities on sailboat racing in the nation, describes in his book *Cornelius Shields on Sailing* what he considers the most important single principle of successful racing: *"The helmsman does not assist the progress of the boat through the water, he impedes it!"*

When you move the helm to keep the boat on her course, you are actually using the rudder as a brake. In theory, the boat travels at her fastest speed when she is sailing herself, and the rudder is merely trailing along behind. In practice, however, the boat makes a certain amount of leeway, with a resultant side pressure on the rudder, and this must be corrected by movement of the helm.

The amount of movement of the helm depends on how the boat is balanced—the relationship between the center of effort of the sails and the center of lateral resistance of the hull. A slight weather helm is desirable so that the boat will have an inherent tendency to work up to windward, but the greater the weather helm the greater the braking effect of the rudder.

It naturally follows that the less you move the tiller the more efficiently you are sailing, and every effort should be made to improve the balance. Try pulling the centerboard up a bit, or moving it aft slightly, and see how it affects the pull on the helm. Moving your live weight a few inches forward or aft can also affect the helm.

The most important element of helmsmanship is the ability to judge the performance of the boat by the feel of the tiller. The slightest change in speed due to sail trim or wind shifts is instantly transmitted through your fingertips. Top-flight skippers have this intangible sensitivity developed to a high degree, and can sail a boat to windward blindfolded.

In fact, I once knew a skipper who was almost totally blind. As with all persons suffering loss of sight, his other senses were highly developed. With his crew serving as eyes, he could outsail everyone on the windward leg and was first around the weather mark in every race he started.

Night sailing is a great help in attaining sensitivity. In the darkness you cannot always see the fluctuations of the telltales, the slight luffing of the sails, or the approaching wave off the bow, and you must rely on the feel of the tiller.

One of the commonest errors of helmsmanship

is pinching—trying to sail too close to the wind when beating. Right after the start of a race the boats are bunched together, and everyone is tensed up to a high pitch, each thinking only of getting his wind clear and being first at the weather mark. Unless you have practiced self-discipline, you'll have a tendency to worry too much about the nearest competitor and try to outpoint him. *Sail your own boat* and keep her footing.

Pinching is especially harmful in strong winds and rough water. Under these conditions, a light-displacement boat will stop dead in the water when you luff. With the increased wind resistance and wave forces shoving her back, her speed through the water is greatly reduced by pinching.

The commonest fault of the beginner is *over-steering*. He invariably tries to steer the boat on an absolutely straight course. Oblivious to slight wind shifts, headers, or lifts, he clutches the tiller tightly in his fist and continually jerks it back and forth. The resultant braking effect of the excessive rudder movement greatly reduces the speed of the boat through the water.

The experienced helmsman neither understeers nor oversteers. With his fingers lightly holding the tiller, his movements are smooth and gradual. All his senses are employed—sight, hearing, balance, and touch. All are attuned to the constantly changing conditions about him. His roving eyes observe everything—the actions of his competitors, the slight fluctuations of the telltales, the darker riffles of a puff of wind on the water up ahead. He hears the faintest change in the sound of the bow waves and feels every variation in the angle of heel.

His boat, figuratively speaking, talks to him through his fingers on the tiller, and he reacts intuitively to every change in the boat's performance. His movements of the helm have but one dominant purpose—to keep the boat traveling at maximum speed.

The basic principle in steering to windward is to bear off when the wind shifts forward and to point up when it shifts aft. The tiller action must be smooth, without sudden jerks, and *prompt*. Any delay in bearing away in a header means loss of speed. Delay in pointing higher in the lifts means loss of distance to windward.

Unfortunately, the skipper has much more on his mind than watching for wind shifts. He must watch his competitors, keep track of their relative positions, and plan his strategy accordingly. A glance at the telltales or masthead fly will tell him how he is pointing relative to the apparent wind, but he really needs an extra pair of eyes. Therefore, his crew should be constantly on the watch for puffs and lulls revealed by dark streaks on the water, calmer areas in the waves, or the actions of boats up ahead, and keep the skipper informed of all changes in wind conditions.

TECHNIQUES IN LIGHT AIR

There is nothing more frustrating to a sailor than racing in light air, and by light I mean a

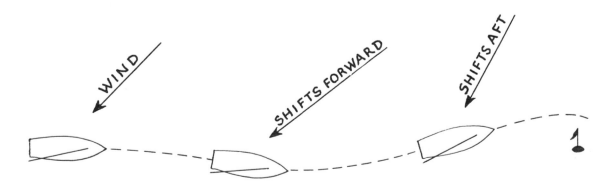

velocity of five knots or less. Tempers flare, there is much cussing about everything in general, and often there is friction between skipper and crew. The alternative is to keep your cool, be patient, and concentrate all the harder on all the factors that control the boat's performance—the set of the sails, balance, weight, skin friction, wind shifts, and interference from competitors.

As I have stated earlier, in light air the mainsail should have a deeper draft than in stronger winds; slack off the outhaul and downhaul, therefore, prior to the start. The jib will have a better shape if the sheet leads are moved inboard a bit, and tension on the luff should be eased.

Balance of the boat is extremely important in light air. Skipper and crew should sit somewhat forward of their normal position to reduce the drag of the stern section. In light air the boat should be heeled to improve the shape of the sails, to insure a light-weather helm, and to reduce the wetted surface and skin friction. Heeling angle should be somewhere between ten and fifteen degrees.

If your boat has a V-bottom or arc-bottom, heeling lifts nearly half of the bottom from the water and drag is greatly reduced thereby. Heeling of all chine-type boats reduces the pounding of the hull on the waves. Boats with round bilges generally point higher in light air when heeled.

Many skippers (myself included) prefer sitting on the leeward side when working to windward in light air. You can see both the windward and the leeward telltales, you get a better picture of the set of the jib, and the flow of wind between the sails is stronger on your face. Steering from the leeward position gives a much more sensitive feel of the boat's performance, and fluctuations of the wind are more readily discernible.

The most important rule for steering to windward in light air is this: *don't point too high.* Pinching robs the sails of their power and drive just when you need these most. As a puff arrives, head up *slowly* and smoothly to increase the boat's speed and gain distance to windward. Then bear off a bit as the puff leaves, so that speed is maintained. Your crew should coordinate the handling of the sheets with your handling of the tiller—trimming as you head up and easing as you bear off. Beware of sheeting the sails too flat or they'll lose their drive—they should be eased off beyond their normal, moderate-wind position.

As I have suggested, hold the tiller lightly in your finger tips so that you can feel or sense the boat's behavior. Bear in mind that the centerboard loses its efficiency as the speed of the boat drops. Therefore, unless you bear off as the wind lightens, the boat will make leeway, and you'll lose all you've gained to windward.

Make every effort to avoid tactical involvement with other boats. Try to keep out of the disturbed air of a group of boats and out of the backwind and blanket zone of the nearest competitor. Normal evasive tactics may not work because you don't have enough speed to maneuver.

To tack or not to tack? The generally accepted rule is to tack when the wind heads you. But in very light air the header may be of short duration, say five or ten seconds. In that case it would be foolish to tack. The best policy is for skipper and crew to be alert for any indication of a *positive* wind shift, such as would be indicated by a dark streak of considerable area ahead and to windward. If another class has started ahead of you, keep an eye on the boats and note the course they are steering. If the majority of them suddenly tack, it is a pretty sure indication that a header of some duration is on the way.

It takes experience and good judgment to decide when to tack for a better wind, particularly if it takes you away from the course toward the next mark. A succeeding wind shift may put your competitors far ahead, or what's worse, in a position to blanket you.

In the final analysis, sailing in light air is just as frustrating to the expert as it is to the novice.

With the elusive wanderings of a fickle wind so difficult to predict, your best bet is to be conservative—don't wander about playing a hunch, and *keep your cool!*

HEAVY WEATHER

To the racing sailor there is nothing more thrilling than beating to windward when it is blowing hard and the seas are kicking up. Pitting your knowledge and skill against the forces of nature is a rewarding experience, and when it is all over, you have a soul-satisfying feeling of accomplishment. Beating your competitors in the process is an added bonus.

But there is one reward that is more lasting: You'll learn more about good seamanship in one heavy-weather race than you will in ten after-noons of batting around in light airs. To be sure, it demands fortitude, concentration, and endurance, but above all else, it's the quality of seamanship that separates the men from the boys.

Proper balance is very important. Skipper and crew should sit well forward to keep the bow down and the stern up. In this position the bow cuts through the waves with least resistance. If the weight is too far aft, the bow slams down into every wave, bringing too much spray aboard, and the excessive pitching and pounding spills wind from the sails.

The rule in heavy-weather sailing is to avoid heeling and keep the boat upright at all times. The only way you can accomplish this is by hiking as far out as you can. Some classes employ the trapeze, and most of them permit the use of hiking straps. Whatever hiking gear your class allows, hike out as far as is humanly pos-

HIKING OUT IN A THISTLE. (*Peter Barlow.*)

sible and keep the boat on her feet. It is a rugged test of endurance, but that's what wins races.

It should be understood that as the speed of a boat increases to near-maximum hull speed, the greatest drag or resistance is that caused by wave-making. This tendency is increased by heeling and is least when the boat is sailed upright.

Heavy winds demand flat sails. Your outhaul should be tightened to its fullest extent to reduce the depth of the mainsail's draft. Tightening the boom downhaul moves the center of effort forward. This enables the boat to point higher and reduces the weather helm.

If your boat has an adjustable main-sheet traveler, the sheet block should be moved outward. Thus you trim the boom *outward* and *down.* This flattens the sail by taking the twist to leeward out of the upper part.

In high winds the jib has a great tendency to sag, so be sure the luff is taut and straight. As with the mainsail, the sheet leads should be moved outboard.

With strong winds and heavy seas don't try to point too high. Keep the boat footing. You need all the drive possible to shove the boat through the waves. The main sheet should be played constantly to parry the puffs and keep the boat from heeling, particularly when the waves are short and choppy.

When the waves are high and long, more in the nature of big swells, steer a weaving course. Head up going *down* the swell, and bear off to increase speed just before you reach the crest. This may seem a bit unnatural, but it keeps the boat moving at maximum speed.

When a tack seems to be in order, don't be impulsive—analyze the situation earnestly before making a decision. Heavy winds are invariably steady in direction, and a header is the exception rather than the rule. But the wave configuration is constantly changing. Watch for a lull or a smooth spot. Several heavy waves are generally followed by a group of smaller ones.

Tack in the calmer moment, and do it *fast.*

Bear off a bit to get maximum speed, then shove the tiller over hard. The smooth, gradual turn employed in light air can be fatal in heavy wind. The one thing to avoid is stalling, or getting in stays. This inevitably leads to a knockdown or capsizing. Remember, a light-displacement boat does not have the momentum to drive through the water when her sails are luffing. *Speed means control!* In a very strong puff or gust, don't luff up—slack the main sheet to avoid heeling and maintain top speed.

REACHING AND RUNNING IN HEAVY WEATHER

As the wind becomes more abeam, the weather helm becomes more pronounced and heeling increases. Hike out to keep the boat on her feet and to ease tiller pressure. If you can tilt to windward, all the better.

The boom vang is vitally important in these conditions, as it gives the sail a more efficient shape and makes the boat easier to steer. When the sheet is slacked to parry a gust the vang prevents the boom from lifting, and the sail retains its flat shape.

A common hazard in heavy weather, particularly when you are running, is capsizing to windward. This is induced by the action of the head of the sail when it twists around like a bag while the boom cocks way up. Slacking the sheet to prevent the tilt to windward only increases the hazard. The boom vang eliminates this tendency by preventing the twist at the head, flattening the sail, and increasing its driving power.

On a reach in heavy wind, *don't* trim the jib too flat. Ease it out a bit to achieve maximum drive. To parry a strong gust, let out the mainsail, allowing it to luff if necessary, while the jib keeps the boat footing, reduces the weather helm, and lessens the angle of heel.

In very high winds, sheet tending is more important than helmsmanship, and the crew must be alert and responsive every second. There is a constant threat of broaching on a reach, and the sheet tender must recognize and react instantly to the threat. In a broach, the boat does not respond to tiller action, but rounds up toward the wind with an increasing angle of heel, and capsizing is imminent.

The corrective action is to let the mainsheet go entirely. With the mainsail luffing and the jib still drawing, the center of effort moves forward. Thus the pressure of the wind on the jib shoves the bow *away* from the wind, the angle of heel decreases, and the rudder becomes effective. The jib sheet should not be released unless you are in dire distress. The mainsheet should be trimmed back at the earliest possible moment to keep the boat moving and under control.

When you are running in heavy weather, crew weight should be moved aft to raise the bow and prevent it from burying or "rooting." If burying is uncontrolled, it can lead to sailing under, or "pitchpolling." Sometimes you can spill the water from the deck by a slight seesawing of the tiller. A sharp luff might do it, but in a small boat you run the risk of capsizing. The best bet is for the crew to shift aft quickly and to slack both sheets.

The centerboard should be entirely down in these conditions, because it provides greater stability, reduces the boat's tendency to roll, and, by its leverage, lessens the chance of a knockdown. But avoid luffing suddenly with the board all the way down, or you may be out of control and capsize. If you cannot steer a straight course before the wind, the board may be raised *slightly*.

CHAPTER 5

Before the Start

Attitudes toward racing vary with the individual—from the casual to the deadly serious. In my own case, I have found that to be successful I have got to work at it. When a race day rolls around, my preparation begins when I tap the barometer upon arising, to see if any change is indicated since I saw the weather map on TV the night before. From then until race time, all my energies are devoted to preparation. The race comes first—ahead of my business, home, and family. While I might be accused of having a somewhat distorted sense of values, the row of lovely trophies adorning my mantel demonstrate that my attitude has paid off. I have noticed that the skippers who consistently win abide faithfully by the Boy Scout's credo—*BE PREPARED!*

Race day preparations should begin with a council of war. You and your crew should sit down together, analyze all the factors that have a direct bearing on your race strategy, and plan accordingly. With the aids I have previously discussed, you have determined what the weather will be at race time, and are reasonably certain of the wind direction and force to be expected throughout the race.

Consult your tide and current tables and note the times of high and low water, as well as the direction and force of the current that will prevail during the race.

You should obtain a race circular as early as possible, and you and your crew must study it carefully. First, the various courses and marks will be shown and designated by letters or numbers. The committee boat will signal the course to be sailed by displaying these letters or numbers, and they should be memorized by you and your crew. Neither of you will have time to read the circular while maneuvering for the start.

It is also imperative that you both memorize the flag signals. (See International Code Flags and Pennants, page 126.) The International Code answering pennant when flown means "Race Postponed." The code flag "N" means "Race Cancelled." Code flag "S" means "Sail the Shortened Course."

The racing instructions give the order of starts for the various classes, and the starting time for each. *These must be fixed in your mind.* First, the signals for the preceding classes enable you to check your watch with that of the committee. Second, remember that the starting signal of the class immediately preceding yours is *your preparatory signal.*

GETTING READY FOR THE RACE. (*Peter Barlow.*)

The race circular must be aboard when you shove off for the race. This should be the responsibility of your crew, so make certain he has it safely stowed on his person. Finally, be sure the stop watch is fully wound and in working order. This reminder may seem trivial, but from experience I can state with authority that more than one start has been fouled up because the crew forgot this little detail.

With these on-shore preliminaries completed, checked, and double-checked, the next step is to rig up the boat and get under way.

The first step on boarding your boat is to check your gear and equipment and see that it is properly stowed. Have a fixed place for everything, where it is readily accessible and not liable to go adrift. Any gear or assorted junk not absolutely necessary should be left ashore.

PREPARING TO LEAVE THE DOCK. (*Peter Barlow.*)

THISTLES JOCKEYING FOR A START. (*Peter Barlow.*)

Get out your little oil can and lubricate every snap shackle, block, and movable fitting. Cam cleats often "freeze" because of salt water corrosion. See that the telltales are in place on each shroud and are flying freely.

When you bend on the sails, inspect them carefully, even though you went over them last week. Constant vigilance is the only insurance against breakdowns. Check all the sail slides to see if any are coming loose. Flex each sail batten before inserting it to be sure none are cracked— if one should break while you are under way, it could tear the sail.

With all the foregoing preparations completed

to the best of your ability, you should give heed to one of the most important precepts of racing strategy—*get out to the starting area EARLY!* You should be out there sailing *at least* half an hour before the first warning gun is fired.

In every race you'll see some boats leave the dock while the guns are going off. Skippers and crews are yelling at each other in utter confusion, frantically trying to do everything at once, and hoping that Lady Luck will get them up to the line in time to start with their class, more or less. Such an attitude reveals a complete lack of foresight and orderly planning.

Getting under way well in advance of the

race might be termed the "shake-down." Final adjustments of sail trim for maximum drive are made, you and your crew settle down in your normal positions, and the boat is "in the groove." Relaxed and comfortable, you can concentrate all your thoughts on the immediate future.

Alert and observant, you see the true state of wind and weather, and how it is going to affect your race. Is it blowing a bit harder than you had expected? Sail close-hauled and look at your mainsail. Little wrinkles running up from each sail slide along the foot indicate that the clew outhaul should be set up a little harder. If the maximum draft appears to be near the center of the sail, set up on the downhaul.

Take a good look at the luff of the jib. If there are little wrinkles running inward from the lower two or three jib snaps, have your crew sock up on the jib halyard.

As race time nears, keep an eye peeled for the arrival of the committee boat. When it has anchored, and the starting buoy has been set, get over there and check the starting line. Ideally, in a windward start, the line should be squared, or at right angles to the true wind. It seldom is, however, and one end will be favored. A quick luff exactly head to the wind in the middle of the starting line will reveal which end is favored or whether the line is truly square. Try it several times to be sure.

Now sail along the line from the committee boat to the starting buoy and back. Have your crew time this run with the stop watch. In your actual start, it will be important to know exactly how long it takes to run the line, in either direction. Be sure you both remember it.

Check the time remaining before the first warning signal. You may find there's enough time for a few practice starts. However, once that first gun goes off, stay out of the starting area. But don't get too far away. You can learn a lot by watching the starts of the earlier classes. Note which end of the line they choose, and if you spot any mistakes in their tactics, it can help you to correct your own errors.

Finally, keep an eye on the committee boat.

Note the course signals and flag hoist—you can never be sure they won't change.

There is no greater thrill in racing than to be first over the starting line at the gun, with your wind clear. Unfortunately, your competitors all have the same idea, and your well-laid plans often go awry. But it is, nonetheless, an ideal to strive for. If you succeed, you'll have your moment of glory, but if you fail, don't despair—your position *five minutes after the start* is of greater importance.

To be a consistently good starter takes a lot of experience and practice. You must be uncommonly alert and observant—constantly aware of all that is happening around you. You must be able to analyze the maneuvers of your competitors and determine their probable intent. With the relative positions of the boats constantly changing, you must be prepared to react instantly to unexpected situations, taking advantage of every opening that can improve your position.

Captain "Hank" Haff, veteran skipper of America's Cup races in the last century, said, "Yacht racing is a game of give and take—give as little as possible, and take all you can get." To be successful you must be aggressive and self-confident—races are not won by the timid.

THE START TO WINDWARD

In planning your start you should observe these basic precepts:

1. Stay in the starting area after your preparatory signal. If the wind lets up you may find yourself becalmed or too far away to reach the line at the starting signal.

2. Keep your boat traveling at maximum speed. Speed means control and maneuverability. Pinching or loafing along ruins your timing.

3. Pick the spot on the line from which you want to start.

4. Cross the line at maximum speed *on the starboard tack*, so that you'll have the right of way. There are one or two situations where a

LIGHTNINGS OFF ON A WINDWARD START. (*Peter Barlow.*)

port tack start seems indicated, but this should not be attempted unless you have had lots of experience.

There are four different methods of starting. One method is excellent, two are questionable, and the other is terrible.

1. *Sitting on the line.* In this method you sail up close to the line a minute or so before the gun, then slack sheets and sit there with sails luffing. Then the gun goes and you trim sheets and try to get moving. Right there you are a dead duck. Boats to windward of you take your wind and prevent you from gaining speed. Boats to leeward crowd you and establish an overlap. With no forward speed your boat cannot respond to the helm, and you can't get out of the way. If you manage to avoid committing a foul, you can count on being last over the line and in a hopeless position.

2. *Running the line.* Here you sail along the line on a reach during the last half minute, intending to trim sheets and head up across the linc at the gun. This is the beginner's favorite method, and occasionally it has been known to work. But it has several inherent dangers. First, all the boats to leeward are close-hauled. They all have the right of way, since you are the windward boat. Thus, they can—and probably will—force you over the line too soon. Secondly, a strong gust of wind may carry you down the line faster than you expected, and you'll reach the end of the line before the gun goes off.

3. *Approaching from above the line.* In this method you sail along just *above* the line the last fifteen or twenty seconds, then dip down across the line and back just as the gun goes off. Again, you are the windward boat, and the close-hauled leeward boats may crowd you so

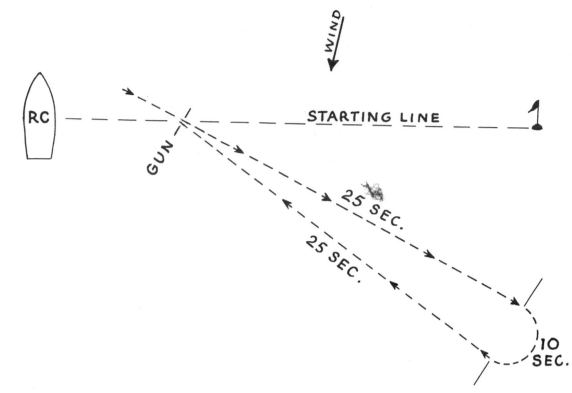

that you cannot dip below the line and round up without fouling. This method is often used by frost-biters or in small-dinghy racing. As a general rule, its use should be restricted to those occasions where there is a fairly long starting line and relatively few starters.

4. *The timed start.* Commonly called the Vanderbilt method, this is the most commonly used and is generally preferred by experts. Under this method, you pick the point on the line at which you wish to start. Then you cross the line from the *wrong* side at this point on a broad reach, noting the time left to go. For most small craft, sixty seconds is ideal. You must know the time it will take under existing wind conditions to complete a 180-degree turn, preferably a jibe. Assuming it is ten seconds, you start the turn at thirty-five seconds to go. Theoretically, this should take you back to the exact spot at which you wish to start just as the gun goes off.

Unfortunately there are variables that may throw you off, such as interference from other boats or wind shifts, and it is difficult to deter-

mine how much time to allow for these factors. A boat on your lee bow can mean trouble, not only because of her backwind but also because of her right to luff you. In order to escape, you should bear away under her stern to get clear wind farther down the line.

The point at which you cross the line is not as important as starting with the gun at maximum speed with your wind clear. If you are too early, slack your sheets to kill speed. To accelerate rapidly, trim your *main* rather than your jib.

BARGING

Simply explained, a boat is barging on a windward start when she approaches the line sailing *below* close-hauled and attempts to force her way between a close-hauled boat on the same tack and the starting mark.

Rule 42.1(e) on Same Tack, Anti-barging Rule, states that when she is approaching the starting line to start, a leeward boat is under no

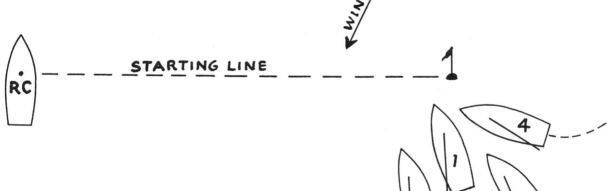

YACHTS 4 AND 5 ARE *BARGING*

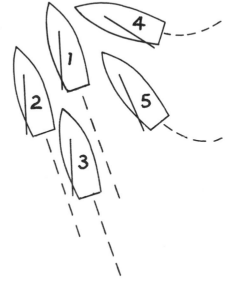

obligation to give any windward boat, overlapping and on the same tack, room to pass on the required side of a starting mark surrounded by navigable water.

If, on the final approach, *before* the starting signal, the leeward boat is forced to bear off to avoid a collision, the windward boat is disqualified. The rule does not apply to boats on opposite tacks, or to boats not overlapping. Barging is not prohibited if it can be done while keeping clear of other boats, but the risks always outweigh the advantages. A skipper who habitually tries a barging start will soon find himself decidedly unpopular!

THE START WITH WIND ABEAM

While most race committees try to avoid them, reaching or running starts are sometimes unavoidable. Here a late start is not very seri-

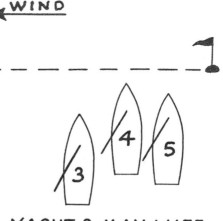

LEEWARD YACHT 1 HAS RIGHT-OF-WAY

YACHT 3 MAY LUFF 4 AND 5 AFTER SHE CROSSES STARTING LINE

ous, since you have greater maneuverability in looking for an opening and a chance to blanket other boats.

As a general rule, try to cross the line near the windward end. If a few boats are to windward of you, they can be luffed as soon as you are over the line. However, if you note a jam at the windward end, start at the leeward end. Here you approach the line on a *close* reach, bearing off to cross the line with the gun.

THE START WITH WIND ASTERN

In this instance *do not* run directly before the wind when it is nearly time for the gun. From the port end, reach along the line nearly parallel to it on the starboard tack and bear away in the last few seconds. As leeward boat, you have the right of way over all boats running directly to the line and may luff them. If you are a little late, you may be able to blanket and pass them. DO NOT set the whisker pole or spinnaker until you are positive you are clear of other starters.

Immediately after the start and the race is on, the whole fleet is generally closely bunched and headed in the proper direction, most of them on the same tack. Let us assume you have made a poor start. You are blanketed, backwinded, wallowing in their wake, unable to point as high, and dropping back. In the belief that, if what you are doing is wrong, the opposite must be right, you split tacks with the fleet and take a long hitch way off by yourself with your wind clear.

This is the classical tactic of the skipper who is inexperienced or lacks confidence in his ability to compete with the leaders. Once in a blue moon it will work, but invariably you'll be last at the windward mark. The preferred tactic is to make a *short* tack to get your wind clear, then go about on your original course. In other words, *stick with the fleet!* If they get a favorable wind shift, you'll get it too. Furthermore, by watching the leading skippers you'll learn the proper use of offensive and defensive tactics.

One important duty of your crew is to keep you informed of the movements of the leading boats. If you know what they are doing and where they are going, you can figure out for yourself the reason for their tactics.

If you are a skipper sailing your first race, these first minutes after the start are the most exciting. Surrounded by boats on all sides, with the accompanying noise and confusion, you are all tensed up and on edge, primarily concerned

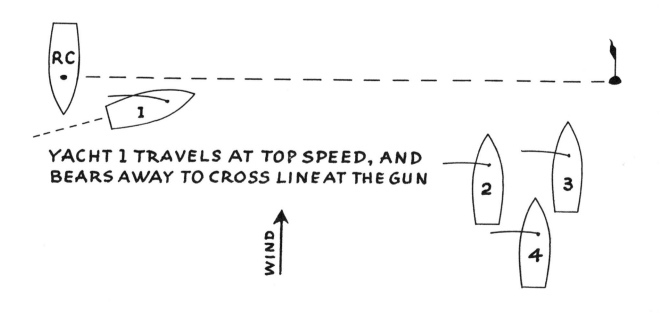

YACHT 1 TRAVELS AT TOP SPEED, AND BEARS AWAY TO CROSS LINE AT THE GUN

WIND

with avoiding a collision. A glance over your shoulder reveals a boat overtaking you to windward. Your natural tendency is to *pinch*—to try to sail closer to the wind to prevent him from passing. But inevitably it fails, and he goes charging by while you drop rapidly astern.

Pinching, or trying to sail too close to the wind, is a common mistake of the beginner, and it is revealed by a slight but continuous fluttering of the luff of the sails. Not being completely full, the sails cannot develop the drive to push the hull through the water, and you'll move sideways more than forward.

The experienced racing skipper draws a fine distinction between *pointing* and *footing,* and knows when to employ each in offensive strategy. He decides whether the circumstances call for steering higher (pointing) than his competitors, or at a greater angle to the wind (footing) with higher speed. The "pointer" sails a shorter course slower, while the "footer" sails a longer course faster.

If two boats start a long hitch together, one pointing and the other footing, the outcome will depend upon the fickleness of the wind and tide. If the wind eventually heads them, the footer will find himself in the lead. If on the other hand they get a "lift," or a more favorable slant, the pointer will be out in front.

Sometimes neither wins. You will often see two boats cross on opposite tacks, one pointing and the other footing, and when they again converge you'll notice that neither has gained.

Occasionally you may find yourself bucking a strong head tide. If, by pinching a bit, you can get it on your lee bow, it will push you up to windward, while the fellow who is footing will gradually sag off.

In very light air, pointing can be fatal. Remember that by footing you actually increase the strength of the *apparent* wind, and you keep your boat moving all the time. To be sure, your increase in speed through the water is very slight, but that small amount could win the race!

In winds that are very puffy, the experienced skipper employs the technique known as "feathering." This is alternately bearing off and pointing higher. It sounds easy, but it requires a high degree of sensitivity, expert timing, and skillful helmsmanship.

The basic requirement of feathering is to begin to head up just *before* the puff hits, and to bear off before it eases and your speed is retarded. Success depends upon your ability to head up or bear away at precisely the correct time. If you delay heading up at a puff, the boat increases her heel and makes leeway. If you delay in bearing off, you lose speed and distance.

In very strong winds feathering is not advisable. If you head up to prevent excessive heeling, you lose so much speed that the boat is less responsive to the rudder and can become unmanageable.

CHAPTER 6

The Beat to Windward

The windward leg might be termed the most critical part of the race. The skipper who reaches the weather mark first will be a hard man to beat, for he is in the enviable position of being in the lead, and is assured of clear air on the ensuing leg.

NO. 109 IS IN A HOPELESS POSITION. (*Peter Barlow.*)

Success on the windward leg is determined by superior helmsmanship and tactics. "Tactics" has been defined as "legal interference with your competitors." When near a competitor you attempt to blanket him, backwind him, and put him in your wake. To be a good tactician, it is imperative that you have a thorough knowledge of the right-of-way rules, and that you know how to play the wind shifts and the current to your advantage.

But before considering tactics, you must have a clear understanding of two critically important situations that can be used both offensively and defensively. First there is the hopeless position.

THE HOPELESS POSITION

When a boat is close-hauled, beating to windward, there is a considerable area of disturbed

HISTLES STARTING THE WINDWARD LEG. (*Peter Barlow.*)

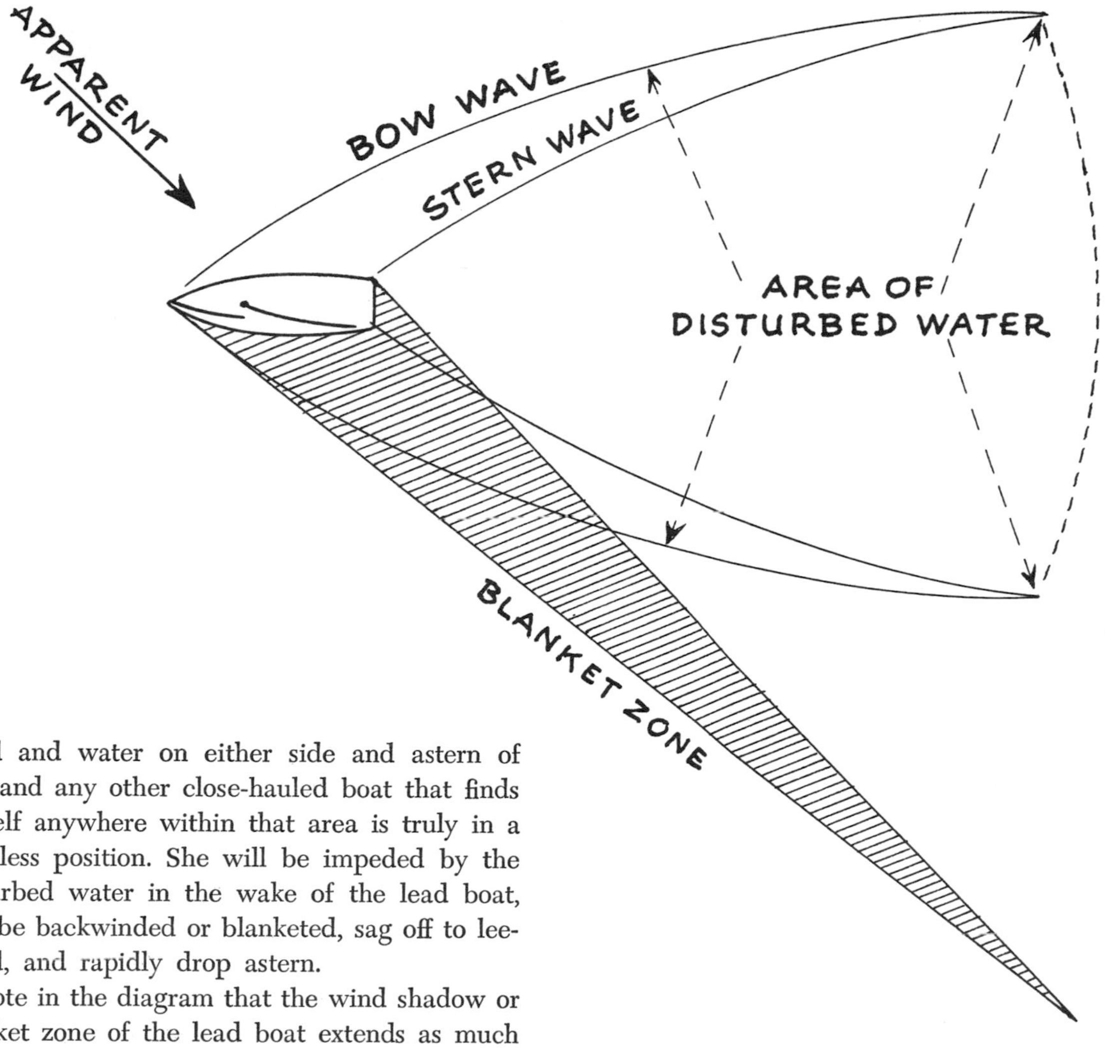

wind and water on either side and astern of her, and any other close-hauled boat that finds herself anywhere within that area is truly in a hopeless position. She will be impeded by the disturbed water in the wake of the lead boat, will be backwinded or blanketed, sag off to leeward, and rapidly drop astern.

Note in the diagram that the wind shadow or blanket zone of the lead boat extends as much as six mast lengths from the boat. Furthermore, the wind is deflected from the sails to a smaller angle of opposition, and a boat astern cannot point as high. This, coupled with the disturbed water caused by the bow and stern waves and the wake, puts her in a very bad spot.

How to escape? If she bears off hoping to break through the wind shadow and disturbed water to get her wind clear, she will have lost so much time and distance to windward that she is practically out of the race. The only solution is to *split tacks at once*. The best tactics, however, are to avoid getting in the hopeless position, and constantly to be on guard against a competitor who might try to force you into such a spot.

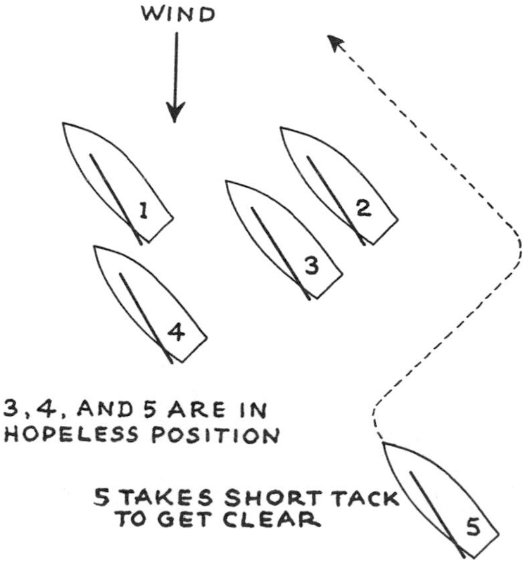

NO. 715 IS IN A SAFE LEEWARD POSITION. (*Peter Barlow.*)

As a complement to the "Hopeless Position," there is the safe leeward berth.

SAFE LEEWARD BERTH

When two close-hauled boats on the same tack are very close to each other and the bow of the leeward boat is ahead of the other, the windward boat is in the *hopeless position,* and the leeward boat is in the *safe leeward berth.*

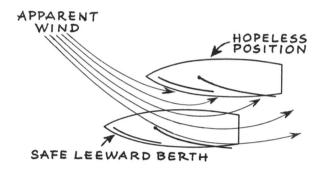

The flow of wind is deflected by the sails of the leeward boat onto the leeward side of the sails of the windward boat, and she is thus effectively backwinded. This deflection and its effect can be increased if the leeward boat trims her mainsail in hard, to throw her backwind more directly against the sails of the other boat.

The disturbed water caused by the bow and stern waves of the leeward boat may extend up to four or five beam widths to windward, and this is an added obstacle to the windward boat since her hull speed is noticeably retarded.

Thus, it is evident that the safe leeward position is the most valuable tactical weapon at your command. You are "safe" because you can protect yourself from a close-following boat by means of your backwind, bow wave, and wake, and because your deflected wind prevents him from passing you to windward. Being ahead, you are first to benefit by a favorable wind shift. Therefore, your strategy should always be to beware of the boats on your lee bow—they can do far more harm to you than boats on your weather bow.

The first and most important prinicple of strategy on the windward leg is to *always take the tack that is closest to the mark!* Where you must make a long tack and a short one to fetch the mark, always make the long tack first. If you get a favorable wind shift, you may be able to lay the mark in one tack. Furthermore, when it is time to take the short tack to the mark, you can more accurately judge if you can lay it, since you'll be fairly close to it.

The second cardinal principle is to *take as few tacks as possible.* Every time you tack you lose valuable seconds, especially in light airs.

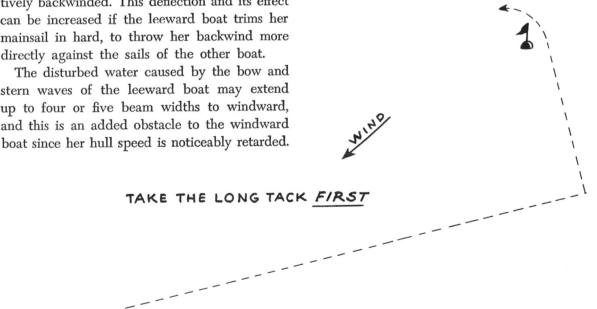

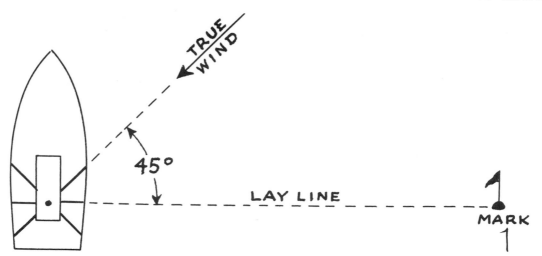

You lose the full driving force of the wind while tacking, your rudder acts as a brake while turning, and you lose time and distance in regaining maximum speed.

LAY LINES

On the windward leg, decisions as to *when* to tack can be arrived at more accurately and quickly by the use of lines painted or taped on the deck, on each side of the cockpit from the helmsman's position. One line is placed on each side deck at *right angles* to the centerline.

The average boat tacks through 90 degrees —which is to say she sails close-hauled at 45 degrees to the true wind. Therefore, sighting along the painted line shows when you have reached the lay line. In other words, when the mark appears on the extension of the line, you tack. This is standard procedure under ideal conditions. But if the wind is very light, or the tidal current is against you, carry on a bit more before tacking to allow for those conditions.

A second pair of lines should be placed on the deck diagonally, at 45 degrees to the centerline, as shown in the diagram. These lines are helpful in several ways.

Let us assume you are on the port tack and another boat, on the starboard tack, is converging with you. Sight along your starboard 45-degree line. If the other boat is on the extension of the line, you are on a *collision course*, and will have to tack to clear him or bear off to pass astern of him.

But note this—if the other boat is to *leeward* of the line, you are ahead of him. Thus, you can go about when you are close under his lee, putting him in the hopeless position and yourself in the safe leeward berth!

Sighting *aft* along the 45-degree line on the

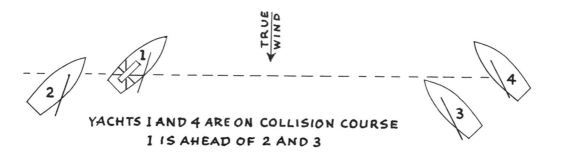

YACHTS 1 AND 4 ARE ON COLLISION COURSE
1 IS AHEAD OF 2 AND 3

weather side will reveal your position relative to your competitors on the same tack. Any boat to *windward* of the extension of the line is *ahead* of you, and you have a lead over any boat to leeward of the line.

Note also that the windward bow line is parallel to the *true* wind, and a glance at your telltale will reveal the approximate difference between the angles of the true and apparent winds.

CHAPTER 7

Rounding the Windward Mark

All during the beat to windward you should be planning your approach to the mark and how you are going to round it. Your tactics will depend on two factors—the nearness of your competitors, and whether the mark is to be passed to port or starboard.

Here is where it is vitally important that you have a clear-cut understanding of the right-of-way rules! More fouls are committed rounding marks than in any other part of the race. When a traffic jam appears to be building up near the mark, you should be able to recognize at a glance the respective rights of each boat and to choose and execute the proper tactic to meet the situation without delay.

When the mark is to be passed to port, *approach the mark on the starboard tack*. Thus, you have the right of way and can round without

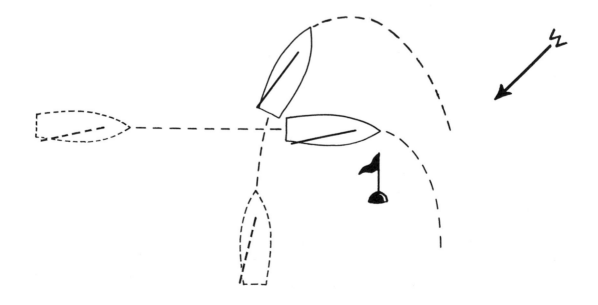

COMING UP TO THE WINDWARD MARK. (*Peter Barlow.*)

tacking. This final tack should not be a long one for the closer you are to the mark the easier it is to determine that you can fetch it. If you start the tack more than fifteen or twenty boat lengths away, you are taking an unnecessary risk—you may get a header or the wind may let up, and you'll sag off below the mark. It is good strategy to overstand the mark a bit, particularly

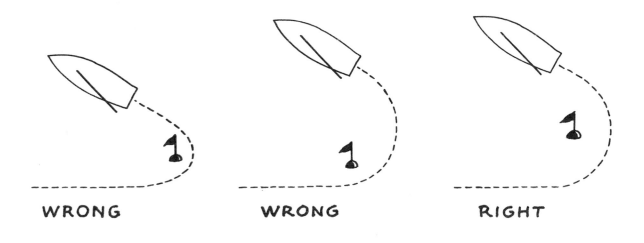

WRONG   WRONG   RIGHT

if there are other boats near you. It is embarrassing to discover that you can't quite fetch the mark and are unable to tack because of boats on your weather quarter.

Many beginners believe that you should *always* approach the mark on the starboard tack, since this is the "right-of-way" tack. This is a mistaken impression for there is one noteworthy exception, and this is a point on which experts disagree.

When the mark is to be passed to *starboard,* it might be advisable to approach on the *port* tack. Thus, you might pass between the stern of a starboard-tack boat and the mark, thereby preventing him from tacking. If you were to approach on the starboard tack, you would have to

come about at the mark. But if a boat is coming up to the mark on the port tack, you *cannot tack directly in front of him,* even though he must keep clear of you. He would simply bear off a bit, go under your stern, and round the mark ahead of you!

There is a right and a wrong way to round a mark. Most beginners cut too close to the mark and round in too sharp a curve, thus killing the boat's headway. Two things should be uppermost in your mind—you want the inside position at the mark and you wind clear *after* rounding. To insure the inside position, try to establish an overlap on any windward boat *before* you reach the mark. Thus, you are entitled to buoy room and can round before the windward boat.

CHAPTER 8

The Reach

On your final approach to the windward mark, whether the next leg is a reach or a run, *set up your boom-jack tightly* while your boom is inboard and you are still close-hauled. Don't wait until after you have rounded!

THE TECHNIQUES OF REACHING

Remembering the old adage that the shortest distance between two points is a straight line, you might assume that off the wind you should steer a straight course for the next mark. This is an erroneous assumption, and it can be explained very simply.

Your prime objective should be to *increase the average speed of your boat to its maximum.* The boat travels fastest on a course somewhere between wind abeam and close-hauled; in other words, on a close reach. Therefore, you should *bear off* a bit in the puffs or flaws, and *luff* in the intervals as the flaw lets up. You lose nothing when you bear off to leeward in the puffs, but the boat's speed is *greatly accelerated* when you luff closer to the wind as the wind lightens.

You may sail a greater *distance* on a zigzag course, but your *elapsed time will be less* than it

would be if you had sailed a straight course to the next mark. Another advantage of this technique is that by bearing off in stronger puffs, you remain in the zone of higher wind velocity *longer;* and by sailing closer to the wind as it lightens, you reach the next flaw *sooner.*

Another important rule to remember when reaching is to sail the boat as upright as possible. When a boat is sailed in a heeled position her waterline is less efficient, her hull has a greater wetted surface, and the tendency to luff increases. Move your crew aft, as all boats tend to bury their bows when sailing free. The centerboard should be tended carefully. The amount of board down depends on the *speed* of the boat—the higher the speed through the water, the less board is needed.

TACTICS

Compared to the windward leg, tactics on the reach are relatively simple, since this leg is sailed on one tack. It is a well-known fact that it is very difficult to overtake the leading boat on a reach—in fact, he often seems to draw ahead. The reason is that he not only has his

LIGHTNINGS ON A REACH. (*Peter Barlow*.)

wind clear, but more important, he is sailing in comparatively *undisturbed water*. It is very difficult to break through the bow and stern waves of a boat in the lead. Therefore, your most effective defensive tactic is to keep *your competitor always in your wake!*

Keep your eye on him every second—if he attempts to pass you to leeward, bear off a bit before he establishes an overlap. If he tries to pass to windward, luff up before you get in his wind shadow. Your speed will be accelerated and you'll put him in the hopeless position.

THE LUFFING MATCH

Let us assume that a boat attempting to pass you to windward has established an overlap close

aboard (i.e., the two boats, side to side, are less than two boat lengths apart). Under the rules you have the right to luff until head to wind, to prevent him from passing. He must respond by also luffing, since he is required to keep clear. This is the start of a typical luffing match, often of prolonged duration.

It seems rather ridiculous to see two boats luffing far out to windward from their normal course, while the rest of the fleet are busily making time to the next mark. The leeward boat must win the match, for he has the windward boat in the hopeless position. But heed this warning: If the luffing match continues too long, the tables are turned, and the *windward boat* becomes the aggressor!

Eventually the leeward boat must bear off for the mark, and the course changes from a reach to a run before the wind. The windward boat then breaks out his spinnaker and effectively blankets the leeward boat!

PASSING TO WINDWARD

Let us assume you are directly astern of a competitor and fairly close. As long as he can keep you in his wake you cannot overtake him, for you are traveling in disturbed water; and as long as you stay there, you are a dead duck! You must attack, but how?

again, but hold your luff, traveling at accelerated speed on a close reach until you are at least three mast lengths to windward. Then bear off for the mark, and if the maneuver is successful, you should be able to blanket the other boat effectively.

The success of this tactic hinges on the element of surprise. You try to catch your competitor off guard, when his attention is directed elsewhere. If you are too close to him, or he is watching you, he'll immediately respond to your luff to prevent your passing, and you'll be off on a senseless luffing match.

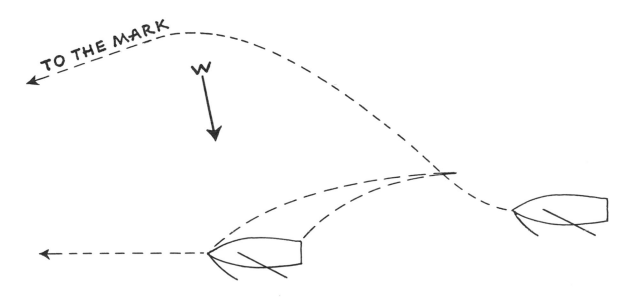

If you try to pass him to leeward, you must break through his bow and stern waves, and then you are in the zone of deflected wind from his sails. If you bear off far enough to avoid being blanketed, you'll be so far to leeward that you'll have lost more than you'll have gained.

Your best offense is to try and break through to windward. The best starting place is from a position *not* directly astern, but rather a bit to windward, and at least three boat lengths back. Watch carefully, and when a strong puff hits, luff sharply, breaking through your competitor's bow and stern waves *precisely where they intersect*. When you are in the clear, *don't* bear off

WHEN YOU ARE BEHIND

Don't give up hope if you are behind on a reach. The odds are in your favor, and you have several things going for you. First, you have your wind clear and undisturbed water. Second, you can profit by the mistakes of those ahead, if you are alert and watchful. They'll be interfering with each other and luffing off the course, wasting time. Steer for the mark. In fact, if you steer slightly *below* the mark, with your course a slight curve rather than a straight line, you'll be close-reaching on your final approach at accelerated speed.

CHAPTER 9

Running Before the Wind

The technique, and likewise the tactics, of running before the wind depends primarily upon the force of the wind. In light to moderate winds you steer a bit to leeward and sail a zigzag course by *bearing off* in the puffs, and luffing in the lulls to accelerate your speed. In strong winds and heavy weather, steer a straight course for the mark.

The first rule to remember is to *heel your boat to windward.* In all but the lightest of airs heeling to windward eases the pull on the tiller and reduces the drag of the rudder.

Glance aloft frequently and keep your eye on the masthead fly. It reveals the apparent wind, is a guide to the proper trim of the spinnaker pole, and tells when you are blanketing a competitor or he is blanketing you.

If you are running in light air, slack off the boom-jack a bit so that the boom can rise and take some of the rigidity out of the mainsail. Likewise, slack off the outhaul to put more draft in the sail.

Many beginners mistakenly assume that the centerboard should be hauled all the way up when running before the wind to reduce drag. While it is true that the less centerboard in the water the better, *some* board is necessary to prevent drift. It is rare that the wind strikes the mainsail at exactly right angles. It is generally slightly over the quarter. If there is no board down, the boat will slide to leeward, or drift.

Drift, even if it is hardly noticeable, retards the boat's speed more than you might suspect. Therefore, when you are sailing before the wind the board should be no more than half or three quarters of the way up. Too much board is better than too little.

Before luffing, jibing, coming about, or setting the spinnaker, *be sure* the board is well down. When you are nearing the leeward mark, and before you take in the spinnaker, see that the board is *all the way* down.

The run is the one leg of the course where the odds are in favor of the boat that is astern. Here the outcome depends entirely upon the skipper, *not* the boat! Here the slowest boat can hold her own with the fastest, if the skipper is on his toes. Blanketing is most effective on the run, for your wind shadow is wider (particularly if you are carrying a spinnaker) and will extend at least four mast lengths to leeward.

Hence it is your greatest weapon of offense, and since your competitors are equally aware of it, be on guard at all times to *keep your wind clear!* If you are threatened by an overtaking boat, harden up, bear off, or even jibe—*anything*

STARS RUNNING BEFORE THE WIND. (*Peter Barlow.*)

is better than being blanketed! And above all, don't get involved in a luffing match . . . on the run it can be fatal!

Let us assume you are overtaking a competitor, and are reasonably sure you can blanket him and pass. *Don't* attempt it **early** in the downwind leg, for once you are ahead you can be certain that he will blanket *you*. It is better to retard your speed and stay on his leeward quarter until *near the mark*. Then you can cross his wake, blanket him, and round the mark in the inside position.

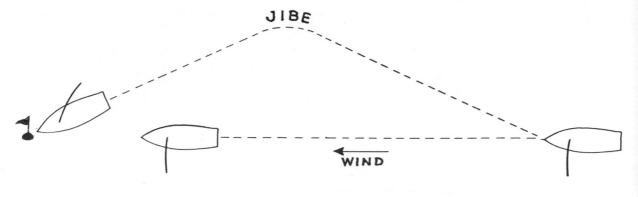

TACKING DOWN WIND

There is one situation where sailing a straight course down wind to the leeward mark may not be the fastest. Let us suppose the wind is extremely light and dead astern. The sails intermit-tently collapse and fill, and the boats barely have steerageway.

By sharpening up about 25 degrees you bring the wind more on your quarter, and you increase your speed by two or three knots. Halfway to the mark you jibe over and sail the rest of the leg on a broad reach. This tactic will work only if the wind is steady in direction and velocity.

CHAPTER 10

The Spinnaker

THE SPINNAKER RUN. (*Peter Barlow.*)

The modern parachute spinnaker can be likened to a fickle woman. It can be inspiring, indispensable, and a magnicent joy to behold. It can also be frustrating, unpredictable, and calamitous. Perfect felicity can only be achieved by ardent devotion and constant, undivided attention. Properly set and trimmed, the spinnaker is your most efficient, and certainly most beautiful sail. A moment's inattention, and it collapses, becoming a hindrance rather than a help.

To the novice, the terms used in describing spinnaker handling can be confusing. Like the jib or mainsail, the spinnaker has a head and a foot, a luff and a leach, and a tack and clew. But on different tacks the terms are interchangeable—the luff and tack, which denote the leading or windward side, become the leach and clew when you are on the opposite tack.

One might say a spinnaker has two "sheets," by which the sail is trimmed to the wind. But that is incorrect—the windward rope controlling the leading edge is the *guy* and is attached to the tack. On the *opposite tack* this rope becomes the *sheet,* and its point of attachment is now the *clew.*

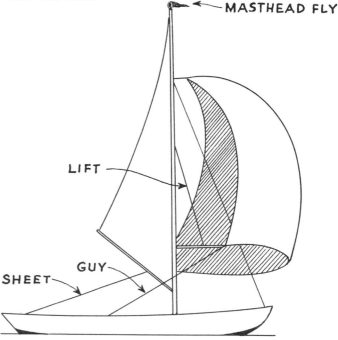

THE EQUIPMENT

The spinnaker halyard should be of braided dacron, with a swivel shackle for attaching to the head of the sail. Keep the shackle well oiled, for if it doesn't turn freely the head of the sail will be twisted.

The "sheets" should likewise be of braided dacron, and most boats carry two sets, one for

the center. When the spinnaker is hoisted the box generally goes overboard, but it is easily replaced.

A clever variation of the expendable container is a large, heavy paper bag. Cut two holes in the bottom, through which the tack and clew may be pulled; the headboard hangs out of the top. When the sheet, guy, and halyard are attached, and the sail is hoisted, the bag tears apart and blows overboard.

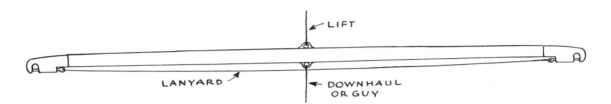

"normal" use, and a very light set for "drifting." The reason for this is that spinnakers are so light in weight that in the very lightest of winds the sheer weight of the sheet could drag down the clew and spoil the set of the sail. Therefore, always carry a set of sheets no larger than an eighth of an inch for those times when the breeze is but a faint zephyr.

Spinnaker pole fittings and gear vary with the size and class of the boat. Basically, the pole end fitting has a quick opening eye that snaps onto the mast fitting and locks automatically. A lanyard is rigged on the underside of the pole attached to the release trigger, and a short pull quickly disengages the pole. A topping lift attached at the center of the pole holds it at an angle of 80–90 degrees upward to the mast. A downhaul of adjustable length holds the pole down when the spinnaker tends to pull it up.

Preparation of the spinnaker is best done at home. It must be stowed in some sort of container, with the headboard on top, and the clew and tack well separated. The simplest container is a corrugated board beer case. Cut slits in the opposite corners on the same side so that the sail corners (tack and clew) may be pulled out of them. The headboard hangs out of the top in

In many small-boat classes, the spinnaker is stowed in a common plastic wastebasket or bucket. Whichever type of container you prefer, stow the sail in it *carefully*. Start by putting the center of the foot of the sail in the box, then pull the foot in evenly until the two tacks hang out about six inches. Continue with the two luffs and accompanying belly until you reach the head. Take heed: Mark the head of the sail with colored twine, dye, or paint of a contrasting color for easy identification. It is rather embarrassing to see the spinnaker go up sideways because you snapped the halyard onto the tack!

A more sophisticated (and more expensive) device is the "turtle." This is a sailcloth bag of ingenious design, with closing flaps. Its main advantage is that the halyard, sheet, and guy can

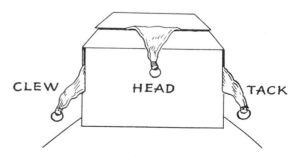

be hooked up in advance and left unattended until you are ready to hoist the spinnaker. Turtles come in a variety of designs by various makers, and in my opinion their advantages outweigh their cost.

If you are not familiar with spinnaker-handling techniques, it is a good idea to rehearse on dry land. Pick a day when the wind is light, and place the boat stern to the wind. Put the spinnaker on the deck, with the tack and the clew well separated. Attach the "sheets" to the tack and clew, and lead them *outside* the shrouds and jibstay, and back to their respective leads, which are on or near the transom. Tie the "sheet" ends together, or make them fast in the cockpit.

Now hoist the spinnaker, with your eye on the head to be sure it doesn't foul. Take note that in light airs the head should be hoisted right to the mast, but in fresh to strong winds it is hoisted to about a foot from the mast. It is good practice to mark the halyard where it is cleated. Then, when racing, you can belay to the mark without having to look aloft to see the position of the head.

Next, snap one end of the spinnaker pole to the corner of the sail, which now becomes the tack. Attach the topping lift and downhaul to the pole, then clip the other end of the pole to its fitting on the foreside of the mast.

Now haul in the sheet and guy until the spinnaker is filled and drawing properly. To test for the correct position, haul in the guy until the luff just starts to shake, then haul in or pay out the sheet until the leech is about to flutter. Now adjust the topping lift and the downhaul.

POSITION OF THE POLE

Here are some cardinal principles of spinnaker tending that should be firmly fixed in your mind, and rigidly adhered to every moment the spinnaker is up. The spinnaker pole should be *perpendicular to the mast at all times*. There are three means of achieving this: (1) by adjusting the topping lift and the downhaul, (2) by raising the slide fitting of the inboard pole end, and (3) by lowering the slide fitting.

The position of the pole has a definite relationship to the foot of the spinnaker. Think of the spinnaker as an isosceles triangle, whose base is the foot of the sail. The foot should be kept *parallel to the water at all times*. As the wind increases the clew will lift, and as it slackens the clew will drop. Therefore, the tack or pole end must be raised or lowered to keep it the same height from the water as the clew. You control this by adjusting the topping lift, downhaul, and mast slide.

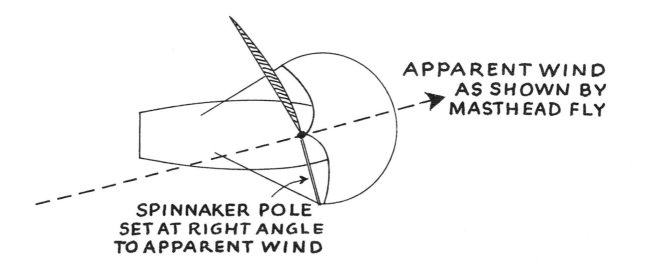

APPARENT WIND AS SHOWN BY MASTHEAD FLY

SPINNAKER POLE SET AT RIGHT ANGLE TO APPARENT WIND

TRIMMING THE GUY

The correct trim of the guy is of vital importance. Bear in mind this important rule: The spinnaker pole must be trimmed *perpendicular to the apparent wind.* If the pole is allowed to go *more* than 90 degrees to the apparent wind, a considerable part of the spinnaker is blanketed by the mainsail. The masthead fly gives the truest indication of the apparent wind, *not* the telltales on the shrouds. Frequent glances aloft will reveal fluctuations in the apparent wind direction, and you must trim the guy accordingly, with not a second's delay.

TENDING THE SHEET

It should be noted that in keeping the spinnaker working at its maximum efficiency, most of the work is done with the sheet, rather than with the guy. Most beginners tend to haul the sheet in too far, and the spinnaker backwinds the mainsail.

The sheet should be eased out until the sail is on the verge of luffing. In strong puffs the sheet should be eased well out, far enough to spill the wind.

The sheet tender must be alert, diligent, and capable of reacting instantly. He must ease and trim the sheet continually to meet the constant shifts of wind. His eyes must be always on the luff. If the luff starts to fold in or collapse, a quick jerk on the sheet, bringing it in a foot or more, will unfold or open the collapsing luff.

In light airs the spinnaker tends to swing or oscillate, which in turn encourages luffing or collapsing. This can be prevented by hauling the halyard in to the limit, with the head of the spinnaker right up to the mast, while at the same time you are trimming in the sheet.

Now that you have familiarized yourself and crew with the operation of the spinnaker on dry land, the next step is to try it afloat, so that you can learn how to operate as a team.

Again pick a day when the wind is very light. Before you get under way, the spinnaker is stowed in its container carefully, clew and tack well separated, headboard on top. The sheet and guy are rigged outside the shrouds and jibstay and shackled to their respective corners, *after* the spinnaker has been placed on deck near the mast, on the side that will be the *windward.*

When you are under way, pay off the main sheet and steer directly before the wind. Since we are considering the small boat sailed by a skipper and a crew of one, their respective duties must be clearly understood, and the following procedures should be executed rapidly. The whole idea is to get that spinnaker set as quickly and smoothly as possible.

The skipper stands up astride the tiller and steers with his knees, freeing both hands to hold the sheet and guy.

Leaning forward from the cockpit, the crew passes the weather jib sheet behind his head so that when the spinnaker is hoisted it is outside the running rigging. He then shackles the halyard onto the headboard and hoists away, watching aloft as it goes up to be sure it does not foul on anything. Meanwhile, the skipper trims in the sheet and guy to "square" the spinnaker.

Without luffing or bearing away, the skipper passes the spinnaker pole to the crew. The crew then shackles the pole to the tack, hooks on the topping lift and downhaul, and pushes the pole out as the skipper pays out the guy. The crew then hooks the pole end to the mast fitting.

The skipper hauls in the guy and sheet until the spinnaker is properly set, while the crew adjusts the height of the pole correctly by means of the downhaul.

The crew sees that the centerboard is about one third down, then overhauls the running gear (halyard, sheet and guy, and jib sheet). He then takes the sheet and guy from the skipper and trims the spinnaker to the optimum setting as was practiced on dry land. That means the pole at right angles to the apparent wind and

SETTING THE SPINNAKER. (*Nancy Graham.*)

the tack and clew the same height from the water.

In light air the guy should be cleated. The skipper sits on the leeward side, and the crew to windward where he can keep one eye on the luff of the spinnaker and the other on the masthead fly. Playing the sheet continually, the crew keeps the spinnaker luff at a favorable angle of incidence.

JIBING THE SPINNAKER

There are several methods of jibing the spinnaker, and the larger the boat and the bigger the crew the more involved the procedure be-

comes. But for the purpose of this book, we are concerned only with the small boat sailed by the skipper and crew of one.

At the start, let it be understood that jibing in strong winds is very hazardous, requiring much training, perfect teamwork, and precise timing. My advice is *don't try it*. Not until you have had a lot of experience behind you, and many hours of sailing with a crew you know you can depend on.

The average small boat can be jibed without the crew getting out on deck. The added weight up forward would contribute greatly to the instability of the boat.

The first step is for the skipper to put the boat dead before the wind and then jibe the

1.
DETACH SPINNAKER
POLE FROM MAST

2.
SNAP POLE TO
OTHER CORNER
OF SAIL

3.
AS MAINSAIL JIBES,
RELEASE POLE FROM
OLD CORNER

4.
ATTACH POLE TO
MAST ON NEW
SIDE

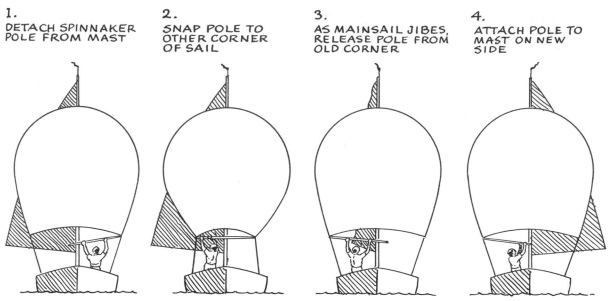

mainsail. The crew then hands the skipper the sheet and guy. The skipper steers with his legs, standing astride the tiller. The crew now unclips the pole from the mast and passes it across forward of the mast, and at the same time the skipper slacks off the sheet and guy, which now become the guy and sheet.

The crew now snaps the free end of the pole to the former clew, which is now the new tack, then unsnaps the other end of the pole from the former tack and hooks it to the mast fitting. The skipper quickly trims the spinnaker and hands the sheet and guy to the crew.

TAKING IN THE SPINNAKER

The boat is sailed directly before the wind, and as before, the skipper stands astride the tiller, steering with his legs. The crew now hands him the sheet and guy.

The crew detaches the pole from the mast, detaches the topping lift and downhaul, and unsnaps the pole from the tack. The skipper immediately lets the sheet fly, and with his free hand takes the pole from the crew and stows it inside the boat.

The crew quickly hauls in the guy until he can reach the tack, then gathers the foot of the spinnaker in *to windward.* Casting off the halyard, he hauls the sail into the cockpit. He then unsnaps the halyard and makes it fast, then unsnaps the sheet and guy and overhauls them.

It should be noted that the centerboard should be lowered *before* the spinnaker is taken in. In a two-man boat this is generally attended to by the skipper.

This is but one of a number of ways to take in the spinnaker. Some skippers prefer lowering on the *leeward* side, in which case the *guy* is let fly to collapse the sail and the sheet is hauled in in the lee of the mainsail. If you are carrying the spinnaker on a reach, this method is preferable. But on a run before the wind, taking it in on the windward has certain advantages. It prevents the sail from flying out to touch a boat to leeward, permits your getting closer to the mark before lowering, and keeps the crew on the weather side.

SPINNAKER HANDLING IN HEAVY AIR

Even under the most ideal conditions, the spinnaker is a very tricky sail to handle, requiring constant, undivided attention, and considerable expertness. But as the wind increases in strength, the spinnaker becomes more difficult to control and is then a potential cause of disaster.

Broaching and capsizing are the inevitable result of carrying the spinnaker in winds that are too strong. In the first place, it is almost impossible to hold a straight course downwind in a small boat with heavy wind. The great leverage of the mainsail when it is broad off causes the boat to luff in the puffs continually, and the rudder cannot hold her straight. This is a common cause of capsizing.

When a strong puff or sudden wind shift endangers the boat, let the sheet fly *immediately* to spill the wind from the spinnaker. Never let the guy go or the sail will *really* foul things up.

In heavy air you must steer an absolutely straight course, dead before the *apparent* wind. If you can't, take the spinnaker down immediately. The centerboard should be lowered part way for more stability, and to make the rudder more effective.

The bow has a tendency to bury in heavy airs, so the skipper and crew should sit somewhat aft of their normal positions. Luffing and then bearing away to lift the bow can result in instant capsizal. If you bear away to the extent that you sail by the lee, there's a very good chance of capsizing to *windward*.

In the final analysis, the spinnaker is and always has been a *light-weather sail*. If, in an effort to beat the other fellow, you insist on flying it in heavy winds, you are displaying poor judgment and bad seamanship.

TAKING IN THE SPINNAKER. (*Nancy Graham.*)

CHAPTER 11

The Finish

As you near the finish line, and you realize the race is nearly over, you look about you and take stock of your situation. To your dismay, you see a bunch of hot-rodders up ahead, and you are way back in the ruck or perhaps last. Your morale takes a sudden drop because things haven't worked out the way you had planned, and for a fleeting moment you wonder if the race was worth all the effort. *DON'T GIVE UP!* Bear in mind that many races are won (or lost) just a few yards from the finish line.

To quit just because you are last is poor sportsmanship and shows that you have the wrong attitude. Don't be discouraged. Be aggressive and keep trying until you are across the line. The leaders may go off on a luffing match, while Tail-end Charlie slips across ahead of them. A sudden wind shift may catch the lead boats on the wrong tack, while you can lay the line with no lost time.

FINISHING TO WINDWARD

Here your primary objective is to take the tack that gives the shortest distance to the line.

Therefore, it is imperative that you determine as early as possible which end of the line is nearer. A common error is overstanding or failing to tack the instant you can fetch the nearest part of the line.

Remember the fundamental rule of tactics—stay between the following competitors and the line. If a boat is close behind you, tack the instant he tacks, to blanket or cover him. If there is a favorable wind shift, you'll get it before he does.

FINISHING OFF THE WIND

The tactical rule just mentioned is fundamental, but be careful not to get in the wind shadow of a following boat or let yourself be blanketed. If you plan to blanket and pass a leading competitor, wait until you are near the finish line—so that he, in turn, cannot do the same to you.

There may be an occasion where all the boats are nearing the finish line on the port tack. One tactic that is often successful is to head up a bit, then jibe after you cross the wind axis, thus gaining starboard tack right of way. Don't attempt it, however, if you are running to leeward of the fleet.

Don't forget that increased speed is gained by sailing at a greater angle to the wind. Thus, if you plan early enough, you may keep somewhat to leeward to finish on a broad reach at accelerated speed.

CROSSING THE FINISH LINE. (*Peter Barlow.*)

CHAPTER 12

Sportsmanship and the Proper Attitude

It has long been my contention that of all the competitive sports, yacht racing demands the highest degree of sportsmanship. In basketball, baseball, and other sports, every move of every contestant is under the watchful eye of a referee or umpire, from start to finish.

But in yacht racing, your "referee" is a race committee on an anchored boat, who can observe only the start and the finish. A few minutes after your starting gun you are out of range of the committee's eyes, and they are not even looking at you. From now on you are on your own, honor-bound to referee your own conduct honestly. If you knowingly violate any one of the racing rules, you must withdraw from the race *at once* and report it to the race committee —*even though the foul was not observed by anyone else!*

If a competitor commits a foul, intentionally or otherwise, and it is observed by you, you must report it to the committee and file a protest immediately after finishing the race. If you fail to do so, you are encouraging poor sportsmanship.

Occasionally you'll find a skipper with the wrong attitude. First, there's the type who ignores a competitor's infractions of the rules be-cause his opponent happens to be a "swell guy." Or perhaps he's afraid that if he protests his friends, they will call him a "sea lawyer."

At the extreme end there's the one who knows the rules forward and backward and uses that knowledge to force a timid or less knowledge-able skipper deliberately into a position where he *cannot avoid* committing a foul. Winning races by means of protest is a poor way to win friends and influence people.

Fortunately for the sport, the characters of this kind are few and far between. Experienced skippers know that the racing rules are designed to protect everybody and to insure competition of the highest order. Thorough knowledge of the rules can be used as both an offensive and a defensive weapon, and most racing tactics are based on that knowledge.

Therefore, it naturally follows that if you want to be a successful skipper you *must* know the rules. This means constant study and observation. In any given situation you must be able to tell at a glance which boat has the right of way and what rule applies. And you must have foresight. If you or a competitor luffs, bears off, jibes, or tacks, *who then* has the right of way?

Equipped with proficiency in boat handling,

and having a working knowledge of a variety of related subjects, you can go out there and race and have a lot of fun. But if you want to *win races,* these skills will get you nowhere unless you first *know the rules.*

For many years I was deeply involved in the activities of a club whose prime purpose was to promote sailboat racing for juniors, and one incident stands out in my memory that graphically illustrates what I have been trying to explain.

It was the last race at the end of a long summer, and the chips were down—this race would decide the season's championships in the various classes. For one twelve-year-old boy it was in the bag. He was so far ahead in points that even if he finished third or fourth in this race he would still take the class championship. I remember how he grinned from ear to ear as he crossed the starting line with the gun, almost beside himself in sheer happiness.

While he was on the long beat to the windward mark in his little 12½-footer, the race committee were busy getting the other classes off. A short time later, when they had time to relax, they were astounded to see the lad coming back downwind from the windward mark.

After a suspenseful wait, he passed close to the committee boat, and with tears streaming down his face he quavered, "Sir, I fouled the southwest mark!"

Now the whole point of this poignant tale is that *no one saw him* touch the buoy. He could have continued the race with no one the wiser (and many a boy would have), but the principles of good sportsmanship had been so implanted in his mind that he did the honorable thing, even though it cost him a championship.

That, my friends, is what I call the Proper Attitude!*

---

* Under the 1969 changes in the rules, a yacht touching a mark is not disqualified providing she corrects her error by rerounding in the approved manner. See new rules 45 and 52.1.

CHAPTER 13

Racing Boats, Including Multihulls

Choosing a racing boat is a matter of deciding which class offers the type of competition you desire. The dominant factors are age and experience. A ten-year-old wants to race against kids his age, and a fifty-year-old would feel embarrassed in a class predominantly raced by teenagers.

As an example of how this is taken care of in one class, the Blue Jays are raced in three divisions. Sailors under fifteen race in the Midgets, over fifteen but under eighteen are in the Junior division, and the Open division takes care of the old fogies.

A beginner in racing, be he young or old, should start in a small one-design-class boat that is simply rigged, stable, and easy to handle. After a couple of seasons' experience, he'll have gotten all he can out of the boat and will be ready to move up to a boat with higher performance, where the competition is of higher caliber.

The reason for beginning with a boat suited to your abilities should be obvious. The object in all racing is to win. But if you start racing in a class where the skippers are all experienced experts, it can be mighty discouraging to finish last in every race. Furthermore, you'll learn more and progress more rapidly if you race with those whose experience and abilities match your own.

For the athletically inclined, the high-performance, lightweight, planing-type boats are popular, such as the Jet 14, O.K. Dinghy, or Flying Dutchman. Some planing boats, notably the International Tempest, employ a trapeze. Very fast and exciting to race, they require expert handling, and the crew must be agile and mentally alert and have instant reflexes.

The most spectacular racing boats are the catamarans, which are unlike anything else that sails. In a strong breeze they take off at fantastic speeds, and the harder it blows the faster they go. They have inherent characteristics unlike those of any other boat, and an experienced sailor needs a little practice to handle them properly.

One of the requirements for active participation in one-design-class racing is yacht-club affiliation. The recognized yacht clubs provide the facilities and conduct the races. Aside from the social aspects, and meeting with people who have a common interest, your membership provides activities for you and your family's enjoyment, and insures their continuance for youngsters of the next generation.

In the final analysis, if you are choosing your first racing boat, you would be wise to consider only those that have a strong, active class organization in the area in which you'll be sailing. If a class is consistently gaining popularity in your area, under enthusiastic, aggressive leadership, you can be assured of satisfying competition and maximum fun.

At the other extreme, if you were to buy into a class that is dwindling in numbers locally, you might end up owning an "orphan" that would have a very low resale value.

ALBACORE

Length overall 15′
Beam 5′4″
Draft 4′9″ centerboard down
Sail area 125 square feet
Weight 300 pounds

The Albacore is a fast, high-performance planing dinghy, of fiberglass or molded plywood construction, depending on the builder, and has built-in flotation. Having a forward deck, she is a dry boat, and can be used as a family day sailer for up to four adults. She is easily trailered and launched. A good boat for training, and carries a spinnaker.

Grampian Marine, Ltd.
451 Woody Road
Oakville, Ontario, Canada

AQUA-CAT

Length overall 12'2"
Beam 6'
Maximum draft 2'
Sail area 90 square feet
Weight 160 pounds

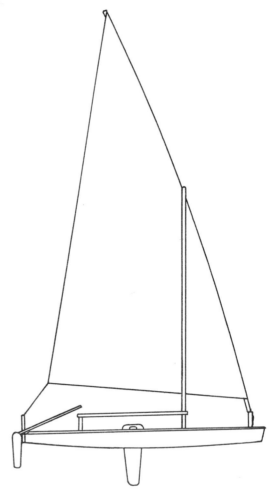

Designed for family fun or exciting competition, this catamaran is easy to sail and safe for youngsters. Her fiberglass hulls are foam-filled, and she's light enough to be cartopped. In racing she has been clocked at over eighteen knots. With sail removed she can be converted to an outboard. Class organization numbers over three thousand in the United States.

American Fiberglass Corporation
Rockland Road
Norwalk, Connecticut 06856

BARNEGAT 17

Length overall 16'7''
Length at waterline 16'2''
Beam 6'
Sail area 145 square feet

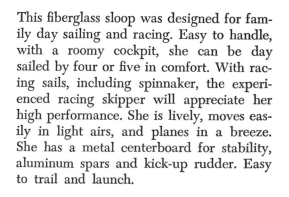

This fiberglass sloop was designed for family day sailing and racing. Easy to handle, with a roomy cockpit, she can be day sailed by four or five in comfort. With racing sails, including spinnaker, the experienced racing skipper will appreciate her high performance. She is lively, moves easily in light airs, and planes in a breeze. She has a metal centerboard for stability, aluminum spars and kick-up rudder. Easy to trail and launch.

Siddons and Sindle, Inc.
17 Central Avenue
Island Heights, New Jersey 08732

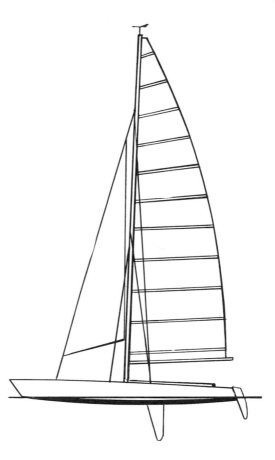

B LION

Length overall 20′
Length at waterline 19′
Beam 10′
Maximum draft 2′6″
Sail area 235 square feet
Weight 420 pounds

The B Lion is a sloop-rigged racing catamaran with a full-battened, high-aspect-
ratio mainsail and pivoting aluminum mast.
The fiberglass hulls have kick-up centerboards and rudders. The connecting crossbeams are hinged in the middle so that the
craft can be folded for trailering. Designed
to International Class B specifications, the
B Lion has won several championships. A
custom trailer is available.

American Fiberglass Corporation
Rockland Road
Norwalk, Connecticut 06856

BLUE JAY

Length overall 13'6"
Beam 5'2"
Draft 3'6" centerboard down
Sail area 90 square feet
Weight 275 pounds

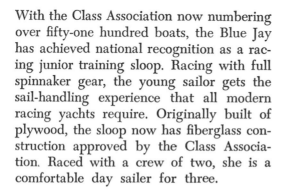

With the Class Association now numbering over fifty-one hundred boats, the Blue Jay has achieved national recognition as a racing junior training sloop. Racing with full spinnaker gear, the young sailor gets the sail-handling experience that all modern racing yachts require. Originally built of plywood, the sloop now has fiberglass construction approved by the Class Association. Raced with a crew of two, she is a comfortable day sailer for three.

McNair Marine, Inc.
Killingsworth Road
Route 81
Higganum, Connecticut 06441

CATFISH

Length overall 13'2"
Beam 6'
Weight 190 pounds
Sail area 105 square feet
Crew capacity 300 pounds

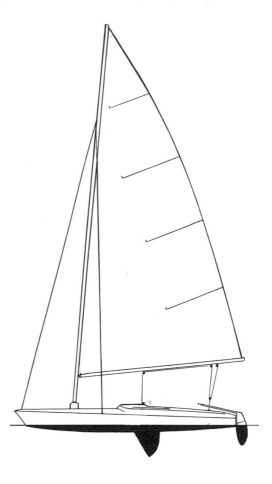

The Catfish is an all-fiberglass catamaran. While she may be used for family fun, she was primarily designed for one-man racing. Heeling and hiking at eighteen or twenty knots provide plenty of thrills. She has built-in flotation, free-feathering aluminum mast, and flip-up rudders. She can be cartopped or trailered, and can be launched, rigged, and ready to sail in under five minutes.

AMF Alcort
P.O. Box 1345
Waterbury, Connecticut 06720

DC-14 P

DC-14 PHANTOM

Length overall 14'2"
Beam 7'
Sail area 140 square feet
Weight 350 pounds

The DC-14 is a high-performance sloop-rigged catamaran for fun sailing or racing. The fiberglass hulls and aluminum spars have foam flotation. The mainsail has full-length battens, and the mast is rotating. Has trampoline lounge deck of Dacron, with raised seats each side. Rudders are raised or lowered by pushing or pulling the tiller. The hulls are detachable for car-topping. She has excellent stability, great speed, and is very easy to sail.

Duncan Sutphen, Inc.
342 Madison Avenue
New York, New York 10017

ENSIGN

Length overall 22'6"
Length at waterline 16'9"
Beam 7'
Draft 3'
Sail area 290 square feet
Weight 3000 pounds

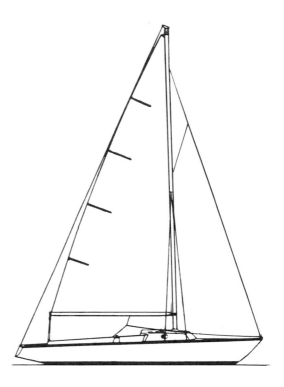

With forty-two fleets and fifteen hundred boats in the national class association, the Ensign has proved to be an outstanding racing day sailer. Strictly one-design, this all-fiberglass keel sloop is fast, able, and easy to handle. With a large cockpit and a moderate sail area, she is a very comfortable family day sailer. Under the cuddy cabin and foredeck are two berths and a toilet for overnight or weekend cruising, and foam flotation is provided throughout. An outboard motor can be carried on a transom bracket, and the boat is trailable. As a family boat of maximum utility, the Ensign is one of the best.

Pearson Yachts
West Shore Road
Portsmouth, Rhode Island 02871

ENTERPRISE
(NATIONAL)

Length overall 13'3"
Beam 5'3"
Draft 3'7"
Sail area 113 square feet
Weight 230 pounds

The Enterprise is a high-performance racing dinghy, with a double-chine hull built of wood or fiberglass. Hers is the largest one-design dinghy class in Great Britain, with over two thousand registered. She is very fast, gets on a plane very easily, and is unsinkable. She is raced with a crew of two and can be day sailed with four. Has three cubic feet of stowage space under the foredeck. Kits are available in various stages of completion.

National Enterprise Company
507 Fifth Avenue
New York, New York 10036

FD

FLYING DUTCHMAN

Length overall 19'10"
Beam 5'7"
Draft 3'8"
Sail area 200 square feet
Weight 375 pounds

An Olympic Class two-man centerboarder, the Flying Dutchman is a high-performance racing boat with a planing hull. She employs a trapeze, carries a spinnaker, and attains very high speeds. She is available in either fiberglass or molded plywood construction, and has built-in flotation. The International Class was organized in 1955, and has over four thousand registered owners.

Siddons and Sindle, Inc.
17 Central Avenue
Island Heights, New Jersey 08732

FJ

FLYING JUNIOR

Length overall 13'2"
Length at waterline 12'3"
Beam 5'3"
Maximum draft 34"
Sail area 100 square feet
Weight 259 pounds

The Flying Junior is one of the fastest growing one-design junior racing classes, with twenty-one hundred registered in the United States and seven thousand worldwide. With a simple main and jib rig, this is a very popular club boat for junior training and racing, and is easily trailered. She is fast, lively, and fun to sail. Of one-piece fiberglass construction, she has a self-bailing cockpit, positive foam flotation, and is unsinkable. Spars and centerboard are aluminum, and she has roller reefing.

Paceship, division of
Industrial Shipping Company, Ltd.
Mahone Bay, Nova Scotia, Canada

FⴤS

FLYING SCOT

Length overall 19'
Length at waterline 18'4"
Beam 6'9"
Maximum draft 4'
Sail area 190 square feet

The Flying Scot is one of the finest family day sailer-racers for her size. Her fiberglass hull has positive flotation, and with her very wide decks can be capsized and righted, often without the crew getting their feet wet. She has hard bilges and sufficient beam so that she can be planed without resorting to acrobatics or a trapeze. A 200-square-foot spinnaker is carried, and class rules permit a crew of two, three, or four. There is ample room for six when day sailing. She is very stable, easy to handle, and very fast. Among the accessories listed as available is a genuine "Glengarrie" Scottish bonnet.

Gordon Douglass Boat Company, Inc.
P.O. Box 28
Oakland, Maryland 21550

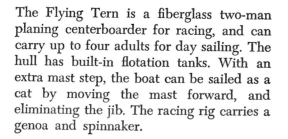

FLYING TERN

Length overall 14′
Beam 5′3″
Draft 3′ centerboard down
Sail area 120 square feet
Weight 286 pounds

The Flying Tern is a fiberglass two-man planing centerboarder for racing, and can carry up to four adults for day sailing. The hull has built-in flotation tanks. With an extra mast step, the boat can be sailed as a cat by moving the mast forward, and eliminating the jib. The racing rig carries a genoa and spinnaker.

Annapolis Boat Rentals, Inc.
P.O. Box 1669
Annapolis, Maryland 21404

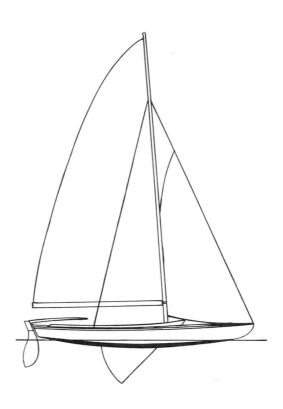

HAMPTON

Length overall 18'
Length at waterline 14'
Beam 5'9½"
Maximum draft 3'6"
Sail area 190 square feet
Weight 500 pounds

The Hampton is the largest one-design racing class on the Chesapeake Bay. She is a hard-chine V-bottom sloop available in either cedar-planked, plywood, or molded fiberglass construction. She is a lively, fast boat, sailed with a crew of one to four. No spinnaker is carried, but a trapeze is used when racing. Having a large cockpit, she is a good boat for day sailing. Kits are available for home finishing.

BOW Manufacturing
P.O. Box 279
Hampton, Virginia 23369

HELLCAT MARK III S

Length overall 25′
Beam 14′
Maximum draft 3′6″
Sail area 300 square feet

This big C class catamaran is affectionately called the "King of the Cats." The hulls are cold-molded plywood, and the beams and spars are aluminum. Cockpit is terylene reinforced with aluminum tubes. Like her smaller sister, the Hellcat, she folds in the center to a five-foot width for easy trailering. While she has a generous sail area, reefing is unnecessary in all but the severest conditions. She is perfectly safe, roomy, and easy to handle as a family boat, yet has the high performance so desirable for racing.

Alleman Enterprises
5819 South Shandle Drive
Mentor, Ohio 44060

HIGHLANDER

Length overall 20'
Beam 6'8"
Draft 4'10" centerboard down
Sail area 225 square feet
Weight 550 pounds

Designed for racing or family day sailing, the Highlander is a decked centerboarder available in fiberglass or molded plywood. She carries a spinnaker, and class rules permit a crew of three or four, but as a day sailer she has ample room for six or seven. Her hard bilges give good stability, and her flat after sections help her plane easily. Kits are available for the home builder. She can be trailered easily.

Douglass and McLeod, Inc.
P.O. Box 311
Painesville, Ohio 44077

INTERLAKE

Length overall 18'
Length at waterline 15'
Draft 4'8" centerboard down
Sail area 175 square feet
Weight 650 pounds

The Interlake is one of the oldest one-design class sailboats in America. Originally built of wood, she was converted to fiberglass in 1955. With her V-bottom and hardchine, she has excellent stability, and the rocker to her keel adds to her weatherliness in steep seas. She is a good family day sailer, and safe for kids or beginners. She has built-in flotation and six hundred pounds of reserve buoyancy when full of water. The aluminum mast and boom are foam-filled. Most of the racing fleets are in the Midwest.

Customflex, Inc.
1817 Palmwood Avenue
Toledo, Ohio 43607

|4

INTERNATIONAL 14

Length overall 14′
Beam 5′5″
Minimum weight 225 pounds
Maximum sail area 125 square feet

Strictly a development class, this world-famous planing dinghy has been radically improved through the years, and there are over two thousand registered, world-wide. Now available in fiberglass construction, she has acquired an impressive racing record in this hottest of all restricted open-class planing dinghies. She flies a spinnaker, and with her very light weight you can expect a very exciting performance in a breeze. She can be cartopped as well as trailered.

W. D. Schock Company
3502 South Greenville Street
Santa Ana, California 92704

JET 14

Length overall 14'
Beam 4'8"
Draft 4'2" centerboard down
Sail area 113 square feet
Weight 165 pounds

The Jet 14 is a high-performance, one-design racing sloop with a planing hull, now available in fiberglass. Lively and very fast, she is extremely sensitive to helm and weight changes. She is raced with a crew of two who must be mentally alert, with instant reflexes, to get the maximum performance. She carries a spinnaker, and the hull has flotation tanks. She can be cartopped, and is easily trailered. For the young racing skipper who wants to train for international competition, this is the boat.

Siddons and Sindle, Inc.
17 Central Avenue
Island Heights, New Jersey 08732

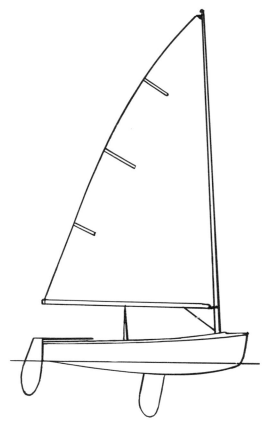

KITE

Length overall 11′7″
Beam 5′
Sail area 78 square feet
Weight 160 pounds

The Kite is a lively little sailing dinghy for family fun. Large enough to be sailed or raced by one or two adults, she can be handled easily by the youngsters. The fiberglass hull has foam flotation and is unsinkable. The flexible spruce mast, patterned after the Olympic Finn, is unstayed and can be quickly stepped and rigged. The boat can be cartopped as well as trailered. An excellent singlehander for the teenager.

Newport Boats
1919 Placentia
Costa Mesa, California 92627

LEADER

Length overall 14′
Length at waterline 13′
Beam 5′5″
Maximum draft 3′6″
Sail area 118 square feet
Weight 230 pounds

The Leader is a double-chine, plywood centerboard sloop, used for day sailing and racing in the Great Lakes area and Canada. A good fun boat for a couple of adults or youngsters. She carries a spinnaker, and is a smart sailer, easily handled. Kits are available for the home builder.

Croce and Lofthouse Sailcraft, Ltd.
4226 Kingston Road
Toronto, Ontario, Canada

LIDO 14

Length overall 14′
Beam 6′
Draft 4′3″
Sail area 111 square feet
Weight 300 pounds

The Lido 14 is a fiberglass sloop for family day sailing or racing. She has a molded deck and fore-and-aft seats, with built-in flotation. An ideal trainer or first boat for a youngster, she can carry up to six persons safely, and is a smart, lively sailer. She has anodized-aluminum spars and a loose-footed mainsail.

W. D. Schock Company
3502 South Greenville Street
Santa Ana, California 92704

LIGHTNING

Length overall 19'
Length at waterline 15'3"
Beam 6'6"
Draft 4'11"
Sail area 117 square feet; with spinnaker,
 300 square feet

One of the most popular of her size, this boat of the International Class has over ten thousand registered owners. Of V-bottom construction, she is available in either fiberglass or wood. She carries a spinnaker, and class rules specify a racing crew of three. With excellent stability, a large cockpit, and plenty of stowage space under the deck, she is a fine day sailer. She is very easy to handle, and can carry up to five people for relaxed sailing with safety.

Siddons and Sindle, Inc.
17 Central Avenue
Island Heights, New Jersey 08732

L 16

LUDERS 16

Length overall 26′4″
Length at waterline 16′4″
Beam 5′9″
Draft 4′
Sail area 260 square feet
Displacement 2950 pounds

The classic L-16 is a racing yacht designed for International competition. Of molded fiberglass, with long overhangs, ballast keel, and minimum wetted surface, she is fast, close-winded, and very responsive to the helm. The cockpit has room for six, and there are two bunks below for overnight trips. Hardware and equipment are top quality. She can be trailered for interfleet competition.

Continental Plastics Corporation
2011 Placentia
Costa Mesa, California 92627

M-20

Length overall 20'
Length at waterline 16'
Beam 5'8"
Maximum draft 3'6"
Sail area: 167 square feet; with
spinnaker, 342 square feet

The M-20 is a molded fiberglass tunneled
hull racing scow with twin bilgeboards. In
the one-of-a-kind series she proved to be
the fastest sailboat of her size, excluding
catamarans. While there is a National class
organization, the majority of the boats are
raced in the Midwest. They carry a spinnaker, and race with a crew of two. With
a large cockpit and deck, the M-20 is a
good day sailer for four or five. She has
built-in flotation, and is easily trailered.

Melges Boat Works, Inc.
Zenda, Wisconsin 53195

MERCURY

Length overall 18'
Length at waterline 13'
Beam 5'4"
Draft 3'1"
Sail area 277 square feet
Weight 1125 pounds

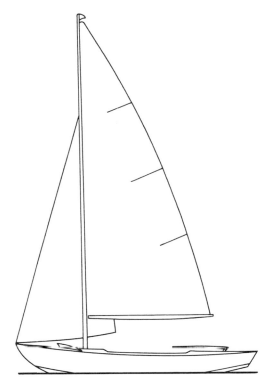

The Mercury is a hard-chine keel boat popular on the West Coast for racing and day sailing. She is a smart sailer, easily handled, and very seaworthy in rough, choppy waters. With 635 pounds of outside ballast, she has excellent stability for relaxed sailing. While she is raced with a crew of two, she can be day sailed comfortably with four. Her hull is fiberglass and spars are spruce.

W. D. Schock Company
3502 South Greenville Street
Santa Ana, California 92704

MOBJACK

Length overall 17'
Length at waterline 16'9"
Beam 6'6"
Sail area 180 square feet
Weight 460 pounds

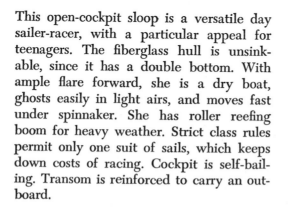

This open-cockpit sloop is a versatile day sailer-racer, with a particular appeal for teenagers. The fiberglass hull is unsinkable, since it has a double bottom. With ample flare forward, she is a dry boat, ghosts easily in light airs, and moves fast under spinnaker. She has roller reefing boom for heavy weather. Strict class rules permit only one suit of sails, which keeps down costs of racing. Cockpit is self-bailing. Transom is reinforced to carry an outboard.

Newport Boats
1919 Placentia
Costa Mesa, California 92627

O. K. DINGHY

Length overall 13′1½″
Length at waterline 12′4″
Beam 4′7¾″
Sail area 90 square feet
Minimum weight 158½ pounds

This high-performance one-man planing dinghy offers exciting competition to the experienced racing enthusiast. The class has six hundred and thirty registered owners in the United States, and about six thousand world-wide. Her principal characteristics are a very light, compartmented hull, and an unstayed, bendy mast. Extremely lively and sensitive, she takes off on a plane at thrilling speeds. Construction is composite—plywood and fiberglass—and kits are available for the home builder. With her simple rig and light weight, she is easily cartopped.

Westin's Boat Shop
River Road
Sayville, New York 11782

110

110
(INTERNATIONAL)

Length overall 24'
Length at waterline 18'
Beam 4'2"
Draft 2'9"
Sail area 167 square feet

The 110 is a keel sloop designed specifically for racing. Organized in 1939, the International 110 class now numbers over seven hundred. Double-enders with a flat bottom and a 300-pound fin keel, the majority are of plywood construction, but class rules now permit the use of fiberglass. They have good initial stability, are close-winded and smart sailers. Styrofoam blocks are fitted for flotation, and the boat may be sailed even when full of water. A trailer can be had to transport the boat from port to port.

Graves Yacht Yards
P.O. Box 36
Marblehead, Massachusetts 01945

P

PACIFIC CAT

Length overall 18′9″
Beam 7′11″
Draft 2′11″ centerboard down
Sail area 267 square feet
Weight 540 pounds

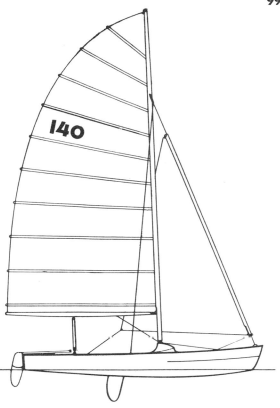

The Pacific Catamaran is one of the fastest one-design boats in the country. It has been clocked at better than twenty knots. The class organization has fleets on both coasts and in Hawaii. The spars are aluminum and the mainsail has full-length battens. One excellent feature is a roller luff-spar, which permits the jib to be reefed under way. The fiberglass hulls have foam flotation, and kick-up rudders for easy beaching.

Newport Boats
1919 Placentia
Costa Mesa, California 92627

PENGUIN

Length overall 11′6″
Length at waterline 11′2″
Beam 4′6″
Sail area 72 square feet
Minimum weight 135 pounds

The International Penguin Class Dinghy Association now has over eight thousand registered owners in the United States and South America. Although the boat was originally designed for plywood construction, the class has approved fiberglass hulls and the two types now race on an even footing. In the New England area the Penguin is popular among some clubs for frostbiting. Being entirely open and light in weight, she is primarily suited for day sailing and racing in sheltered waters rather than heavy weather and rough seas. She is light enough to be cartopped.

McNair Marine, Inc.
Killingsworth Road
Route 81
Higganum, Connecticut 06441

RAINBOW

Length overall 24'2"
Length at waterline 17'3"
Beam 6'3"
Draft 3'6"
Sail area 278 square feet

The Rainbow is a fiberglass, fin-keel, racing day sailer. With a masthead rig and permanent backstay, this sloop has an 1120-pound fin keel for stiffness and high-performance sailing. She has aluminum spars, and carries a spinnaker. With a large, deep cockpit, she provides comfortable day sailing for most families. Under the cuddy cabin are two berths and a head, so the boat can be used for overnight or weekend cruising.

Ray Greene and Company, Inc.
508 South Byrne Road
Toledo, Ohio 43609

REBEL

Length overall 16'
Length at waterline 14'9"
Beam 6'6"
Draft 3' centerboard down
Sail area 166 square feet
Weight 700 pounds

Now in her nineteenth year, the Rebel is an established racing class. Of molded fiberglass, she is an excellent family day sailer, able, weatherly, and easy to sail. She has foam flotation and self-bailing cockpit. She is available with three deck plans—the Standard has wide deck and open cockpit, the Mark II has a long cockpit and contoured seats, and the Mark III has a molded cuddy cabin. Spars are aluminum and centerboard is steel. The boat is easy to trail, and an outboard bracket can be fitted for auxiliary power.

Ray Greene and Company, Inc.
508 South Byrne Road
Toledo, Ohio 43609

-R-B-

RHODES BANTAM

Length overall 14'
Length at waterline 13'11"
Beam 5'6¼"
Draft: centerboard up, 5½"; center-
  board down, 4'2"
Sail area 125 square feet
Weight 325 pounds

The Bantam is a hard-chine sloop of plywood or fiberglass construction, with aluminum spars. She is an excellent first boat, as
a trainer or day sailer. She is easy to handle, roomy and stable. For racing, there is
optional equipment, such as genoa jib and
spinnaker, boom vangs, hiking straps, and
tiller extension. Fiberglass hull and parts
kits, and prefab mahogany plywood kits
are available. Organized in 1946, the class
numbers over fifteen hundred world-wide.

Customflex, Inc.
1817 Palmwood
Toledo, Ohio 43607

RHODES 19

Length overall 19′2″
Length at waterline 17′8″
Beam 7′
Draft: centerboard model, 4′11″; keel
    model, 3′3″
Sail area 176 square feet

With more than thirty racing fleets, the Rhodes 19 class is one of the largest in the United States. Of fiberglass construction, she is available as a centerboarder for shoal waters, or with a 415-pound keel for blue-water racing. As a day sailer, she has a roomy cockpit for six or seven, and a shelter cabin for overnight trips. Forward deck is ample for spinnaker handling. She has a well in afterdeck for an outboard motor.

The O'Day Company
168 Stevens Street
Fall River, Massachusetts 02722

SHARK ONE-DESIGN AND B CLASS

Length overall 20′
Length at waterline 18′7″
Beam 10′
Sail area 272 square feet
Weight 350 pounds

Shark is the largest one-design catamaran class, and the fastest, with over two hundred and ninety registered in the United States and Canada. Built of fiberglass and aluminum, she is dry, responsive, and very maneuverable. One of her outstanding features is her portability. After the removal of only one bolt, she can be folded to a width of five feet for easy trailering. She has tilting centerboards and four storage compartments. For family fun she is safe and a real thrill to sail.

Alleman Enterprises
5819 South Shandle Drive
Mentor, Ohio 44060

SHIELDS ONE-DESIGN

Length overall 30′2½″
Length at waterline 20′
Beam 6′5¼″
Draft 4′9″
Sail area 498 square feet
Displacement 4600 pounds

This fiberglass keel racing sloop offers the ultimate in one-design competition for the experienced skipper. Her fine lines and long overhangs result in a lively, well-balanced boat that is fast in light weather or a hard breeze. The hull incorporates flotation compartments and watertight bulkheads. Fleets of these boats are in use at the U. S. Naval Academy and the Merchant Marine Academy and Shields has been chosen for numerous intercollegiate competitions.

Chris-Craft Corporation
P.O. Box 860
Pompano Beach, Florida 33061

SKIPJACK

Length overall 14′7″
Beam 5′3″
Sail area 125 square feet
Weight 320 pounds

A high-performance sailing dinghy, the Skipjack is used at the U. S. Naval Academy for its sailing programs. Fiberglass hull and aluminum mast have foam flotation, making her unsinkable. Mainsail has full-length battens. The rounded deck-edges make hiking comfortable, and the cockpit floor is above the waterline, making her self-bailing. She planes quickly, points high, and foots fast. She has enough stability to be used for day sailing or junior training.

Newport Boats
1919 Placentia
Costa Mesa, California 92627

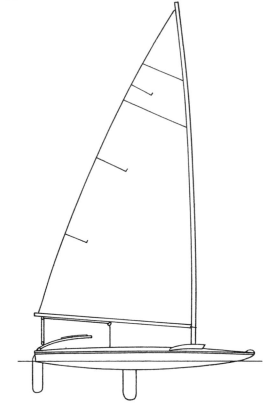

SKYLARK

Length overall 14'2"
Beam 4'8"
Sail area 100 square feet
Weight 260 pounds

The Skylark is a one-design sailing class with a fiberglass tunnel planing hull, having some of the characteristics of a sailing board and a catamaran. She has an unstayed bending aluminum mast and aluminum bilge boards. She has a shallow cockpit for leg room, and can carry three persons. Skylark planes easily, and is exciting to sail or race. She is unsinkable, has excellent initial stability, and can be cartopped.

Starcraft Corporation
P. O. Box 577
Goshen, Indiana 46526

SNIPE

Length overall 15'6"
Length at waterline 13'6"
Beam 4'8"
Sail area 128 square feet
Weight 425 pounds minimum

The most popular small sailboat racing class in the world, the International Snipe Class has over eighteen thousand boats in 503 fleets in twenty-eight countries. Originally she was built of wood to rigid one-design specifications, but class rules now approve fiberglass construction. The Snipe is considered tops as a day sailer and racer for youngsters and the young-at-heart. She is fast, exciting to sail, sensitive to the helm, and performs beautifully under all conditions.

W. D. Schock Company
3502 South Greenville Street
Santa Ana, California 92704

SQUALL

Length overall 9′4″
Beam 4′5″
Sail area 67 square feet
Weight 125 pounds, less equipment

The Boston Whaler Squall is a versatile dinghy of double fiberglass, urethane foam filled, and therefore unsinkable. As a smart, able sailing dinghy she is ideal for the novice as well as the experienced. As a yacht tender she may be rowed from two positions, carry four persons comfortably, and may be powered by an outboard up to 3 hp. The lateen sail has aluminum spars designed to float, and the centerboard is lever-operated and cannot be lost in the event of a capsizal. She has a padlocked locker in the seat aft to stow your lunch or loose gear.

The Fisher-Pierce Company, Inc.
1149 Hingham Street
Rockland, Massachusetts 02370

STAR

Length overall 22'8"
Length at waterline 15'6"
Beam 5'8"
Draft 3'4"
Sail area 285 square feet
Keel weight 900 pounds

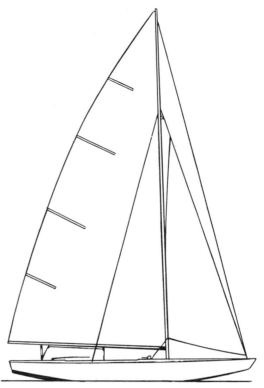

With over five thousand boats registered in the International Class, the world-famous Star offers the highest type of competition for the man who takes his racing seriously. Now in her sixty-first year, this two-man keel boat has been improved and highly engineered to maximum performance. Class rules now allow fiberglass hulls as an alternative to the conventional wood. Stars carry no spinnakers, and as an economy measure you are allowed to buy but one suit of sails a year. The boats are commonly trailered about the country for maximum participation in important series.

Old Greenwich Boat Company
180 Southfield Avenue
Stamford, Connecticut 06902

THISTLE

Length overall 17′
Beam 6′
Draft 4′6″ centerboard down
Sail area 175 square feet
Weight 300 pounds

With over twenty-five hundred owners, in one hundred and twenty-five fleets, the Thistle is one of the best-known racing boats. Built of molded plywood or fiberglass, she is fast and lively, and planes even in light winds. Though the boat is raced with a crew of two or three, the cockpit seats five comfortably as a day sailer, and the flared bow sections keep the boat dry. The cockpit is deep, and you sit down inside on seats with the coaming as a backrest. Building kits are available in various stages of completion. With her light weight and high performance, the Thistle is truly an exciting boat to sail or race.

Douglass and McLeod, Inc.
P.O. Box 311
Painesville, Ohio 44077

TOWN CLASS

Length overall 16'6"
Beam 5'9"
Sail area 152 square feet
Weight 600 pounds

For over thirty years the Town Class has been a popular one-design racing class in clubs along the Atlantic Coast. Now available in fiberglass, this is an able, wholesome design suitable for rough waters and heavy winds. With a 55-pound metal centerboard and a sail plan with a low center of effort, the boat is stiff on her feet and safe for kids or family sailing.

Town Class Boats
Lane's End
Newbury, Massachusetts 01950

210

210
(INTERNATIONAL)

Length overall 29'10"
Length at waterline 24'
Beam 5'10"
Draft 3'10"
Sail area 305 square feet
Displacement 2400 pounds
Ballast 1175 pounds

Organized as a class in 1946, the 210 now has sixteen fleets in the United States and Hawaii. Often called the 110's big sister, the 210 is also a double-ended keel sloop of plywood construction, bronze fastened over oak frames. Styrofoam flotation is provided. The 210 is a sharp sailer, sensitive and responsive to the helm, and provides the highest type of competition.

Graves Yacht Yards
P.O. Box 36
Marblehead, Massachusetts 01945

U. S. MONOTYPE

Length overall 14'2"
Beam 5'8"
Sail area 95 square feet
Weight 240 pounds

The Monotype is a cat-rigged single-hander, a racing boat of high performance for Olympics-like sailing. With weights cut to a minimum, she sails fast, points high, and readily planes in the lightest airs. She has a dagger board, and a portable 25-pound lead ballast to be moved from side to side. Her one-of-a-kind rating is 11.8. Frame kits are available for plywood hulls, and there is a fiberglass version. Spars are spruce.

Ellie's Boat Works
1300 North Betty Lane
Clearwater, Florida 33515

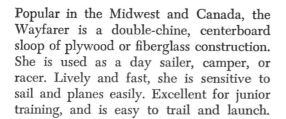

WAYFARER

Length overall 15′10″
Length at waterline 14′10″
Beam 6′1″
Maximum draft 3′10″
Sail area 141 square feet
Weight 365 pounds

Popular in the Midwest and Canada, the Wayfarer is a double-chine, centerboard sloop of plywood or fiberglass construction. She is used as a day sailer, camper, or racer. Lively and fast, she is sensitive to sail and planes easily. Excellent for junior training, and is easy to trail and launch.

Avon Sailboats
1033 East Auburn Road
Rochester, Michigan 48063

WINDMILL

Length overall 15'6"
Beam 4'8"
Draft 4'2", centerboard down
Sail area 119 square feet
Weight 198 pounds

The Windmill is a high-performance one-design racing sloop that has achieved great popularity in recent years, both here and abroad. There are over two thousand registered in the United States, and fleets as far away as Finland. Inexpensive, light in weight, and very fast, she offers exciting competition to the most ardent skipper. Relatively narrow of beam, she might be called an open-cockpit boat, with full-length washboards in lieu of decks. Formerly built of plywood, the Windmill Class has now approved of fiberglass construction.

Durabilt Corporation
Murray Road
Winston-Salem, North Carolina 27106

BEETLE CAT

12'4"×6'×2'6". Sail area 100 square feet. Gaff-rigged. Wood hull and spars. Races with crew of two.

Concordia Company, Inc.
South Wharf
South Dartmouth, Massachusetts 02748

COMET

16'×5'×3'6". Sail area 130 square feet. Fiberglass or wood hull, aluminum or wood spars. Positive buoyancy. Races with crew of two.

Siddons and Sindle, Inc.
17 Central Avenue
Island Heights, New Jersey 08732

C LARK

14'×5'9"×3'6". Sail area 131 square feet, plus spinnaker. Fiberglass hull, aluminum spars. Buoyancy: self-rescuing. Race with crew of two.

Clark Boat Company
18817 East Valley Highway
Kent, Washington 98031

DEMON

15'×5'3"×3'2". Sail area 116 square feet, plus spinnaker. Fiberglass hull, aluminum spars. Buoyancy: self-rescuing. Race with crew of two.

Advance Sailboat Corporation
16400 East Truman Road
Independence, Missouri 64050

C SCOW

20'×6'8"×3'6". Sail area 216 square feet. Cat rig. Buoyancy: self-rescuing. Wood or fiberglass hull, wood spars. Twin bilgeboards. Races with crew of two.

Melges Boat Works, Inc.
Zenda, Wisconsin 53195

DYER DELTA

18'8"×6'1"×4'6". Sail area 189 square feet, plus spinnaker. Fiberglass hull, aluminum spars. Positive flotation. Races with crew of three.

The Anchorage
57 Miller Street
Warren, Rhode Island 02885

CAPE DORY 14

14'6"×4'3"×3'6". Sail area 85 square feet. Cat rig. Weight 250 pounds. Fiberglass hull, aluminum spars. Races with crew of one.

Cape Dory Company
373 Crescent Street
West Bridgewater, Massachusetts 02379

E SCOW

28'×6'9"×4'9". Sail area 319 square feet, plus spinnaker. Wood or fiberglass hull, wood spars. Buoyancy: self-rescuing. Races with crew of three. Has twin bilgeboards.

Melges Boat Works, Inc.
Zenda, Wisconsin 53195

EXPLORER

17′×6′4″×4′6″. Sail area 147 square feet, plus spinnaker. Fiberglass hull, aluminum spars. Positive flotation. Races with crew of two or three.

Sailstar Boats, Inc.
1 Constitution Street
Bristol, Rhode Island 02809

FALCON

15′8″×5′9″×2′10″. Sail area 137 square feet, plus spinnaker. Fiberglass hull, aluminum spars. Positive flotation. Races with crew of two.

Sterling Boatbuilding Corporation
P.O. Box 106
East Greenwich, Rhode Island 02818

FIREBALL

16′2″×4′8½″×4′½″. Sail area 123 square feet, plus spinnaker. Wood or fiberglass hull. Positive flotation. Races with crew of two.

Westin's Boat Shop
River Road
Sayville, New York 11782

5-0-5

16′6″×6′6″×3′9″. Sail area 172 square feet, no spinnaker. Fiberglass or wood hull, aluminum or wood spars. Built-in flotation. Races with crew of two. Trapeze employed.

Royal Sailboats Company
1815 Northwest Boulevard
Columbus, Ohio 43221

420

13′9″×5′5″×3′2″. Sail area 110 square feet, plus spinnaker. Fiberglass hull, wood or aluminum spars. Positive flotation. Buoyancy: self-rescuing. Races with crew of two. Trapeze employed.

Nautica Corporation
P.O. Box 26
Paramus, New Jersey 07652

G.P. 14

14′×5′×3′7″. Sail area 102 square feet, no spinnaker. Wood hull, wood spars. Positive flotation. Races with crew of two.

John Wright, Jr.
328 West Queen Lane
Philadelphia, Pennsylvania 19144

GEARY 18

18′×5′2″×4′8″. Sail area 157 square feet, no spinnaker. Wood or fiberglass hull, wood or aluminum spars. Buoyancy: self-rescuing. Races with crew of two.

Clark Boat Company
18817 East Valley Highway
Kent, Washington 98031

INTERCLUB

11′6″×4′7″×3′5″. Sail area 72 square feet. Cat rig. Fiberglass hull, aluminum spars. Positive flotation. Races with crew of two.

The O'Day Corporation
168 Stevens Street
Fall River, Massachusetts 02722

KOHINOOR

15′3″×6′×4′9″. Sail area 145 square feet, no spinnaker. Wood hull, wood spars. Buoyancy: none added. Races with crew of two.

Wright-built Boat Company
Dundee, New York 14837

LONE STAR 13

13′×5′×3′. Sail area 93 square feet, no spinnaker. Masthead rig. Fiberglass hull, aluminum spars. Has twin bilgeboards, built-in flotation. Races with crew of two.

Chrysler Boat Corporation
1001 Industrial Avenue
Plano, Texas 75074

LONE STAR 16

16′×6′1″×3′10″. Sail area 160 square feet, plus spinnaker. Fiberglass hull, aluminum spars. Positive flotation. Has twin bilgeboards. Races with crew of three.

Chrysler Boat Corporation
1001 Industrial Avenue
Plano, Texas 75074

M SCOW

16′×5′8″×2′8″. Sail area 146 square feet, no spinnaker. Wood or fiberglass hull, wood spars. Twin bilgeboards. Buoyancy: self-rescuing. Races with crew of two.

Melges Boat Works, Inc.
Zenda, Wisconsin 53195

M-16

16′×5′6″×2′6″. Sail area 150 square feet, no spinnaker. Wood or fiberglass hull, wood spars. Buoyancy: self-rescuing. Bilgeboard scow. Races with crew of two.

Melges Boat Works, Inc.
Zenda, Wisconsin 53195

MIRROR DINGHY

10′10″×4′7″×2′9″. Sail area 69 square feet, no spinnaker. Sloop rig. Wood hull, wood spars. Buoyancy: self-rescuing. Races with crew of two.

James Bliss and Company
Route 128
Dedham, Massachusetts 02026

MOTH

11′×4′9″×3′. Sail area 82 square feet. Cat rig. Buoyancy: optional. Fiberglass hull, wood or aluminum spars. Races with crew of one.

Royal Sailboats Company
1815 Northwest Boulevard
Columbus, Ohio 43221

NATIONAL ONE-DESIGN

17′×5′8″×3′6″. Sail area 137 square feet, no spinnaker. Wood or fiberglass hull, wood or aluminum spars. Buoyancy: self-rescuing. Races with crew of two.

Fiberglass Unlimited
8133 Milmont Street
Massilon, Ohio 44646

NIPPER

12′×5′2″×2′8″. Sail area 100 square feet, no spinnaker. Cat rig. Wood or fiberglass hull, wood or aluminum spars. Buoyancy: none added. Races with crew of two.

Ray Greene and Company
508 South Byrne Road
Toledo, Ohio 43609

OMEGA

13′7″×5′4″×3′. Sail area 108 square feet, no spinnaker. Fiberglass hull, aluminum spars. Positive flotation. Races with crew of two.

Wesco Marine
8211 Lankershim Boulevard
North Hollywood, California 91605

OPTIMIST PRAM

8′×4′×2′6″. Sail area 35 square feet. Positive flotation. Wood hull, wood spars. Races with crew of one or two.

Ellie's Boat Works, Inc.
1300 North Betty Lane
Clearwater, Florida 33515

RAVEN

24′2″×7′×5′4″. Sail area 300 square feet, plus spinnaker. Wood or fiberglass hull, aluminum spars. Buoyancy: positive flotation. Races with crew of three.

Cape Cod Shipbuilding Company
Narrows Road
Wareham, Massachusetts 02571

SPARKLER

11'×4'6"×2'6". Sail area 70 square feet, no spinnaker. Buoyancy: self-rescuing. Fiberglass hull, aluminum spars. Races with crew of one.

Ellie's Boat Works
1300 North Betty Lane
Clearwater, Florida 33515

STARFISH

13'8"×4'×2'4". Sail area 82 square feet. Lateen rig. Positive flotation. Fiberglass hull, aluminum spars. Races with crew of one.

Fillip Manufacturing Company
1923 Austin Street
San Angelo, Texas 76901

SUPER SATELLITE

14'×6'×3'6". Sail area 130 square feet, no spinnaker. Fiberglass hull, aluminum spars. Positive flotation. Race with crew of two.

Wesco Marine
8211 Lankershim Boulevard
North Hollywood, California 91605

WINDJAMMER

16'9"×6'6"×4'7". Sail area 158 square feet, no spinnaker. Fiberglass hull, aluminum spars. Buoyancy: self-rescuing. Races with crew of two.

Chesapeake Marine Industries, Inc.
13193 Warwick Boulevard
Newport News, Virginia 23607

Y-FLYER

18'×5'8"×4'. Sail area 161 square feet, no spinnaker. Buoyancy: self-rescuing. Plywood or fiberglass hull, wood or aluminum spars. Races with crew of two.

Glenn Mottin Sailboat Sales and
Manufacturing Company
8005 Monroe, St. Louis, Missouri 63114

COLUMBIA 5.5
32'5"×6'3"×4'4". Sail area 311 square feet, plus spinnaker. Fiberglass hull, aluminum spars. Flotation tanks. Races with crew of three.

Columbia Yacht Corporation
275 McCormick Avenue
Costa Mesa, California 92626

COLUMBIA 21
21'8"×7'7"×3'3". Sail area 234 square feet, plus spinnaker. Fiberglass hull, aluminum spars. Races with crew of two.

Columbia Yacht Corporation
275 McCormick Avenue
Costa Mesa, California 92626

CRESCENT
24'×7'×4'1". Sail area 298 square feet, plus spinnaker. Fiberglass hull, aluminum spars. Racing crew of three.

Customflex, Inc.
1817 Palmwood Avenue
Toledo, Ohio 43607

ORION
19'×6'9"×4'6" (centerboard version available, 1'8" draft). Sail area 200 square feet. Fiberglass hull, aluminum spars. Has positive flotation. Races with crew of two.

Sailstar Boats, Inc.
1 Constitution Avenue
Bristol, Rhode Island 02809

SCHOCK 25
25'×7'×4'. Sail area 222 square feet, plus spinnaker. Fiberglass hull, aluminum spars. Buoyancy: self-rescuing. Races with crew of three.

W. D. Schock Company
3502 South Greenville Street
Santa Ana, California 92704

OTHER RACING BOATS—MULTIHULL CLASSES

A-LION
18′×7′6″×2′6″. Sail area 150 square feet, no spinnaker. Cat rig. Fiberglass hull, aluminum spars. Positive flotation. Raced singlehanded.

American Fiberglass Corporation
Rockland Road
Norwalk, Connecticut 06856

TIGER CAT
17′×7′11½″×3′1″. Sail area 180 square feet, no spinnaker. Fiberglass hull, aluminum spars. Positive flotation. Races with crew of two.

Lippincott Boat Works
Canal Avenue
Riverton, New Jersey 08077

COUGAR MKIII
18′9″×7′11½″×2′8″. Sail area 235 square feet, no spinnaker. Fiberglass hull, aluminum spars. Positive flotation. Races with crew of two.

Rebcats
733 Fifteenth Street N.W.
Washington, D.C. 20016

TORNADO
20′×10′×2′6″. Sail area 235 square feet, no spinnaker. Wood hull, fiberglassed. Aluminum spars. Buoyancy: self-rescuing. Races with crew of two. Employs trapeze.

Alleman Enterprises
5819 South Shandle Drive
Mentor, Ohio 44060

PHOENIX
18′×7′11″×2′8″. Sail area 220 square feet, no spinnaker. Fiberglass hull, aluminum spars. Employs trapeze. Positive flotation. Races with crew of two.

Gibbs Boat Company
LaSalle, Michigan 48145

TRIUMPH 24
Trimaran—24′×14′×3′. Sail area 242 square feet, no spinnaker. Fiberglass hulls, aluminum spars. Positive flotation. Races with crew of two.

Lasco Marine
Hope Street
Alviso, California 95002

SHEARWATER
16′6″×7′6″×5′. Sail area 235 square feet, no spinnaker. Fiberglass hull, aluminum spars. Employs trapeze. Positive flotation. Races with crew of two.

McNichols Boat Sales
1617 East McNichols Street
Detroit, Michigan 48203

CHAPTER 14

The Yacht Racing Rules Including Team Racing Rules of the International Yacht Racing Union as Adopted by the North American Yacht Racing Union

NOTE:

In translating and interpreting these rules, it shall be understood that the word "shall" is mandatory, whereas the word "should" is directive and not mandatory, and the words "can" and "may" are permissive.

Right of way when not subject to the racing rules

The rules of Part IV do not apply in any way to a vessel which is neither intending to race nor racing; such vessel shall be treated in accordance with the International Regulations for Preventing Collisions at Sea or Government Right-of-Way Rules applicable in the area concerned.

Part I, Definitions, has been removed from this portion of the North American Yacht Racing Union's Rules and incorporated in the **Glossary of Sailing Terms.**

PART II

MANAGEMENT OF RACES

Authority and Duties of Race Committee

The rules of Part II deal with the duties and responsibilities of the race committee in conducting a race, the meaning of signals made by it and of other actions taken by it.

1—General Authority of Race Committee and Judges

1. All races shall be arranged, conducted and judged by a race committee under the direction of the sponsoring organization, except as may be

provided under rule 1.2. The race committee may delegate the conduct of a race, the hearing and deciding of protests or any other of its responsibilities to one or more sub-committees which, if appointed, will hereinafter be included in the term "race committee" wherever it is used.

2. For a special regatta or series, the sponsoring organization may provide for a jury or judges to hear and decide protests and to have supervision over the conduct of the races, in which case the race committee shall be subject to the direction of the jury or judges to the extent provided by the sponsoring organization.

3. All yachts entered or racing shall be subject to the direction and control of the race committee, but it shall be the sole responsibility of each yacht to decide whether or not to start or to continue to race.

4. The race committee may reject any entry without stating the reason.

5. The race committee shall be governed by these rules, by the prescriptions of its national authority, by the sailing instructions, by approved class rules (but it may refuse to recognize any class rule which conflicts with these rules) and, when applicable, by the international team racing rules, and shall decide all questions in accordance therewith.

2—Notice of Race

The notice of a race or regatta shall contain the following information:

(a) That the race or races will be sailed under the rules of the International Yacht Racing Union (I.Y.R.U.) and the prescriptions of the national authority concerned.

(b) The date and place of the regatta and the time of the start of the first race and, if possible, succeeding races.

(c) The class or classes for which races will be given.

The notice shall also cover such of the following matters as may be appropriate:

(d) Any special instructions, subject to rule 3.1, which may vary or add to these rules or class rules.

(e) Any restrictions or conditions regarding entries and numbers of starters or competitors.

(f) The address to which entries shall be sent, the date on which they close, the amount of entrance fees, if any, and any other entry requirements.

(g) Particulars and number of prizes.

(h) Time and place for receiving sailing instructions.

(i) Scoring system.

(j) That for the purpose of determining the result of a race which is one of a series of races in a competition, decisions of protests shall not be subject to appeal if it is essential to establish the results promptly.

3—The Sailing Instructions

1. **Status**—These rules shall be supplemented by written sailing instructions which shall rank as rules and may alter a rule by specific reference to it, but except in accordance with rule 3.2(b) (ii) they shall not alter Parts I and IV of these rules; provided however, that this restriction shall not preclude the right of developing and testing proposed rule changes in local regattas.

2. **Contents**—(a) The sailing instructions shall contain the following information:

(i) That the race or races will be sailed under the rules of the I.Y.R.U. and the prescriptions of the national authority concerned.

(ii) The course or courses to be sailed or a list of marks or courses from which the course or courses will be selected, describing all marks and stating the order in which and the side on which each is to be rounded or passed.

(iii) The course signals.

(iv) The classes to race and class signals, if any.

(v) Time of start for each class.

(vi) Starting line and starting area if used.

(vii) Finishing line and any special instructions for shortening the course or for finishing a shortened course. (Where possible the sailing instructions for finishing a shortened course should not differ from those laid down for finishing the full course.)

(viii) Time limit, if any, for finishing.

(ix) Scoring system, if not previously announced in writing, including the method, if any, for breaking ties.

(*b*) The sailing instructions shall also cover such of the following matters as may be appropriate:

(i) The date and place of the race or races.

(ii) When the race is to continue after sunset, the time or place, if any, at which the International Regulations for Preventing Collisions at Sea, or Government Right-of-Way Rules, shall replace the corresponding rules of Part IV, and the night signals the committee boat will display.

(iii) Any special instructions, subject to rule 3.1, which may vary or add to these rules, or class rules, and any special signals.

(iv) Eligibility; entry; measurement certificate; declaration.

(v) Any special instruction or signal, if any, regarding the carrying on board and wearing of personal buoyancy.

(vi) Names, sail numbers and letters, and ratings of the yachts entered.

(vii) Any special instructions governing the methods of starting and recall.

(viii) Recall numbers or letters, if used, of the yachts entered.

(ix) Time allowances.

(x) Length of course or courses.

(xi) Method by which competitors will be notified of any change of course.

(xii) Information on tides and currents.

(xiii) Prizes.

(xiv) Any special time limit within which, and address at which, the declaration that all rules have been observed, if required, or written protest shall be lodged, and the prescribed fee, if any, which shall accompany the latter.

(xv) Time and place at which protests will be heard.

(xvi) That for the purpose of determining the result of a race which is one of a series of races in a competition, decisions of protests shall not be subject to appeal if it is essential to establish the results promptly.

(xvii) Whether races postponed or abandoned for the day will be sailed later and, if so, when and where.

(xviii) Disposition to be made of a yacht appearing at the start alone in her class.

3. **Distribution**—The sailing instructions shall be available to each yacht entitled to race.

4. **Changes**—The race committee may change the sailing instructions by notice, in writing if practicable, given to each yacht affected not later than the warning signal of her class.

5. **Oral Instructions**—Oral instructions shall not be given except in accordance with procedure specifically set out in the sailing instructions.

4—Signals

1. **International Code Flag Signals**—Unless otherwise prescribed in the sailing instructions, the following International Code flags shall be used as indicated:

"AP," Answering Pennant—Postponement Signal.

When displayed alone means:

"All races not started are postponed until later in the day. The warning signal will be made 30 seconds after this signal is lowered."

When displayed over the letter "A" means: "All races not started are postponed to a later date."

When displayed over a class signal means: "The above signals apply to the designated class only."

"B"—Protest Signal.

When displayed by a yacht means:

"I intend to lodge a protest."

"L"—When displayed means:

"Come within hail" or "Follow me."

"M"—Mark Signal.

When displayed on a buoy, vessel, or other object, means:

"Round or pass the object displaying this signal instead of the mark which it replaces."

"N"—Abandonment Signal.

When displayed alone, means:

"All races are abandoned."

When displayed over a class signal, means:

"The designated race is abandoned."

"N over X"—Abandonment and Resail Signal.

When displayed alone, means:

"All races are abandoned and will shortly be resailed. Watch for fresh starting signals."

When displayed over a class signal, means:

"The designated race is abandoned and will shortly be resailed. Watch for fresh starting signals."

"N over First Repeater"—Cancellation Signal.

When displayed alone means:

"All races are cancelled."

When displayed over a class signal means:

"The designated race is cancelled."

"P"—Preparatory Signal.

When displayed means:

"The class designated by the warning signal will start in 5 minutes exactly."

"R"—Reverse Course Signal.

When displayed alone, means:

"Sail the course prescribed in the sailing instructions in the reverse direction."

When displayed over a course signal, means:

"Sail the designated course in the reverse direction."

"S"—Shorten Course Signal.

When displayed alone

(a) at or near the starting line, means:

"All classes shall sail the shortened course prescribed in the sailing instructions."

(b) at or near the finishing line, means:

"All classes shall finish the race either at the prescribed finishing line at the end of the round still to be completed by the leading yacht, or in any other manner prescribed in the sailing instructions under rule 3.2(a)(vii)."

(c) elsewhere, means:

"All classes shall finish between the nearby mark and the committee boat."

When displayed over a class signal, this signal applies to the designated class only.

"1st Repeater"—General Recall Signal.

When displayed, means:

"The class is recalled for a fresh start as provided in sailing instructions."

2. **Signaling the Course**—The race committee shall either make the appropriate course signal or otherwise designate the course before or with the warning signal.

3. **Changing the Course**—The course for a class which has not started may be changed:

(a) by displaying the appropriate postponement signal and indicating the new course before or with the warning signal to be displayed after the lowering of the postponement signal; or

(b) by displaying a course signal or by removing and substituting a course signal before or with the warning signal.

(The race committee should use method (a) when a change of course involves either shifting the committee boat or other starting mark, or requires a change of sails which cannot reasonably be completed within the 5-minute period before the preparatory signal is made.)

4. **Signals for Starting a Race**

(a) Unless otherwise prescribed in the sailing instructions, the signals for starting a race shall be made at 5-minute intervals exactly, and shall be either:

(i) *Warning Signal*—Class flag broken out or distinctive signal displayed.

Preparatory Signal—Code flag "P" broken out or distinctive signal displayed.

Starting Signal—Both warning and preparatory signals lowered.

In system (i) when classes are started:

(a) at 10-minute intervals, the warning signal

for each succeeding class shall be broken out or displayed at the starting signal of the preceding class, and

(b) at 5-minute intervals, the preparatory signal for the first class to start shall be left flying or displayed until the last class has started. The warning signal for each succeeding class shall be broken out or displayed at the preparatory signal of the preceding class, or

(ii) *Warning Signal*—White shape.
Preparatory Signal—Blue shape.
Starting Signal—Red shape.

first class to start

In system (ii) each signal shall be lowered 30 seconds before the hoisting of the next, and in starting yachts by classes, the starting signal for each class shall be the preparatory signal for the next.

(*b*) Although rule 4.4(*a*) specifies 5-minute intervals between signals, this shall not interfere with the power of a race committee to start a series of races at any intervals which it considers desirable.

(*c*) A warning signal shall not be made before its scheduled time, except with the consent of all yachts entitled to race.

(*d*) Should a significant error be made in the timing of the interval between any of the signals for starting a race, the recommended procedure is to have a general recall, abandonment or postponement of the race whose start is directly affected by the error and a corresponding postponement of succeeding races. Unless otherwise prescribed in the sailing instructions, a new warning signal shall be made. When the race is not recalled, abandoned or postponed after an error in the timing of the interval, each succeeding signal shall be made at the correct interval from the preceding signal.

5. **Finishing Signals**—Blue flag or shape. When displayed at the finish, means: "The committee boat is on station at the finishing line."

6. **Other Signals**—The sailing instructions shall designate any other special signals and shall explain their meaning.

7. **Calling Attention to Signals**—Whenever the race committee makes a signal, except "R" or "S" before the warning signal, it shall call attention to its action as follows:

Three guns or other sound signals when displaying "N," "N over X," or "N over 1st Repeater."

Two guns or other sound signals when displaying the "1st Repeater," "AP," or "S."

One gun or other sound signal when making any other signal.

8. **Visual Signal to Govern**—Times shall be taken from the visual starting signals, and a failure or mistiming of a gun or other sound signal shall be disregarded.

5—Cancelling, Postponing, or Abandoning a Race and Shortening Course

1. The race committee:

(*a*) before the starting signal may shorten the course or cancel or postpone a race for any reason, and

(*b*) after the starting signal may shorten the course by finishing a race at any rounding mark or cancel or abandon a race because of foul weather endangering the yachts, or because of insufficient wind, or because a mark is missing or has shifted or for other reasons directly affecting safety or the fairness of the competition.

2. After a postponement the ordinary starting signals prescribed in rule 4.4(*a*) shall be used, and the postponement signal, if a general one, shall be hauled down before the first warning or course signal is made.

3. The race committee shall notify all yachts concerned by signal or otherwise when and where a race postponed or abandoned will be sailed.

6—Starting and Finishing Lines

The starting and finishing lines shall be either:

(*a*) A line between a mark and a mast or staff on the committee boat or station clearly identified in the sailing instructions;

(b) a line between two marks; or

(c) the extension of a line through two stationary posts, with or without a mark at or near its outer limit, inside which the yachts shall pass.

For types (a) and (c) of starting or finishing lines the sailing instructions may also provide a mark at or near the inner end of the line, in which case yachts shall pass between it and the outer mark.

7—Start of a Race

1. **Starting Area**—The sailing instructions may define a starting area which may be bounded by buoys; if so, they shall not rank as marks.

2. **Timing the Start**—The start of a yacht shall be timed from her starting signal.

8—Recalls

1. Yachts' sail numbers shall be used as recall numbers except that the race committee may instead allot a suitable recall number or letter to each yacht in accordance with rule 3.2(b)(viii).

2.(a) When, at her starting signal, any part of a yacht's hull, crew, or equipment is over the starting line or its extensions, or she is subject to rule 51.1(c) and has not returned to the right side of the starting line around one of the starting marks, the race committee shall either:

(i) display her recall number or letter as soon as possible and make a suitable sound, or

(ii) follow such other procedure as may be prescribed in the sailing instructions.

(b) When there is either a number of un-identified premature starters, or an error in starting procedure, the race committee may make a general recall signal in accordance with rules 4.1, "1st Repeater," and 4.7. Unless otherwise prescribed in the sailing instructions, a fresh warning and preparatory signal shall be given. Rule infringements before the preparatory signal for the new start shall not be cause for disqualification.

3. As soon as a recalled yacht has wholly returned to the right side of the starting line or its extensions, the race committee shall so inform her by removing her recall number if displayed; if not, by hail if practicable or in some other manner prescribed in the sailing instructions.

9—Marks

1. **Mark Missing**

(a) When any mark either is missing or has shifted, the race committee shall, if possible, replace it in its stated position, or substitute a new one with similar characteristics or a buoy or vessel displaying the letter "M" of the International Code —the mark signal.

(b) If it is impossible either to replace the mark or to substitute a new one in time for the yachts to round or pass it, the race committee may, at its discretion, act in accordance with rule 5.1.

2. **Mark Unseen**—When races are sailed in fog or at night, dead reckoning alone should not necessarily be accepted as evidence that a mark has been rounded or passed.

10—Finishing

Unless otherwise prescribed in the sailing instructions, in races where there is a time limit, one yacht finishing within the prescribed limit shall make the race valid for all other yachts in that race.

11—Ties

When there is a tie at the finish of a race, either actual or on corrected times, the points for the race for which the yachts have tied and for the place immediately below shall be added together and divided equally. When two or more yachts tie for a trophy or prize in either a single race or a series, the yachts so tied should, if possible, sail a deciding race; if not, either the tie shall be broken by a method established under rule 3.2(a)(ix), or the yachts so tied shall either receive equal prizes or share the prize.

12—Yacht Materially Prejudiced

When the race committee decides that, through

no fault of her own, the finishing position of a yacht has been materially prejudiced; by rendering assistance in accordance with rule 58, Rendering Assistance; by being disabled by another yacht which should have kept clear; or by an action or omission of the race committee, it may cancel or abandon the race or make such other arrangement as it deems equitable.

13—Resailed Races

When a race is to be resailed:

1. All yachts entered in the original race shall be eligible to sail in the resailed race.

2. Subject to the entry requirements of the original race, and at the discretion of the race committee, new entries may be accepted.

3. Rule infringements in the original race shall not be cause for disqualification.

4. The race committee shall notify the yachts concerned when and where the race will be resailed.

14—Award of Prizes, Places, and Points

Before awarding the prizes, the race committee shall be satisfied that all yachts whose finishing positions affect the awards have complied with the racing rules and sailing instructions. It is recommended that the sailing instructions require the member in charge of each yacht to submit within a stated time after she has finished a race a signed declaration to the effect that "all the rules and sailing instructions were obeyed in the race (or races) on (date or dates of race or races)."

(Numbers 15, 16, and 17 are spare numbers.)

PART III

GENERAL REQUIREMENTS

Owner's Responsibilities for Qualifying His Yacht

A yacht intending to race *shall, to avoid subsequent disqualification, comply with the rules of Part III before her preparatory signal and, when applicable, while* racing.

18—Entries

Entries shall be made as required by the notice of the race or by the sailing instructions.

19—Measurement Certificates

Every yacht entering a race shall hold such valid measurement or rating certificate as may be required by the national authority or other duly authorized body, by her class rules, by the notice of the race, or by the sailing instructions and she shall adhere to the conditions upon which such certificate was based.

20—Ownership of Yachts

1. Unless otherwise prescribed in the conditions of entry, a yacht shall be eligible to compete only when she is either owned by or on charter to and has been entered by a yacht or sailing club recognized by a national authority or a member or members thereof.

2. Two or more yachts owned or chartered wholly or in part by the same body or person shall not compete in the same race without the previous consent of the race committee.

21—Member on Board

Every yacht shall have on board a member of a yacht or sailing club recognized by a national authority to be in charge of the yacht as owner or owner's representative.

21A—Crew

1. NUMBER IN CREW—Except as otherwise provided in class rules, the total crew of a yacht, including the skipper, shall not exceed: 2, for yachts with less than 100 square feet of sail area; 3, for yachts with 100 or more, and less than 200, square feet of sail area; and for yachts with 200 or more square feet of sail area, 1 for every 250 square feet of sail area and fraction thereof plus 3. Sail area is the total area entered in a yacht's measurement certificate or otherwise arrived at and used in the final formula determining her rating.

COUNTING WOMEN AS CREW—Except as otherwise provided in class rules, on yachts of more than 25 feet waterline length, women not taking any active part in handling the yacht do not count as crew. On smaller yachts, women count as crew.

22—Shifting Ballast

1. **General Restrictions.** Floorboards shall be kept down; bulkheads and doors left standing; ladders, stairways, and water tanks left in place; all cabin, galley, and forecastle fixtures and fittings kept on board; all movable ballast shall be properly stowed under the floorboards or in lockers, and no dead weight shall be shifted.

2. **Shipping, Unshipping, or Shifting Ballast; Water.** No ballast, whether movable or fixed, shall be shipped, unshipped, or shifted, nor shall any water be taken or discharged except for ordinary ship's use, from 9 P.M. of the day before the race until the yacht is no longer racing, except that bilge water may be removed at any time.

23—Anchor

Unless otherwise prescribed by her class rules, every yacht shall carry on board an anchor and chain or rope of suitable size.

24—Lifesaving Equipment

Unless otherwise prescribed by her class rules, every yacht, except one which has sufficient buoyancy to support the crew in case of accident, shall carry adequate lifesaving equipment for all persons on board, one item of which shall be ready for immediate use.

25—Sail Numbers, Letters, and Emblems

1. Every yacht of an international class recognized by the I.Y.R.U. shall carry on her mainsail:

(*a*) When racing in foreign waters a letter or letters showing her nationality, thus:

A	Argentine	EC	Ecuador
AL	Algeria	F	France
AR	United Arab Republic	G	West Germany
		GO	East Germany
B	Belgium	GR	Greece
BA	Bahamas	GU	Guatemala
BL	Brazil	H	Holland
BU	Bulgaria	HA	Netherland Antilles
CA	Cambodia		
CB	Colombia	I	Italy
CY	Ceylon	IR	Republic of Ireland
CZ	Czechoslovakia		
D	Denmark	IS	Israel
E	Spain	J	Japan

K	United Kingdom	P	Portugal
		PH	The Philippines
KA	Australia	PR	Puerto Rico
KB	Bermuda	PU	Peru
KBA	Barbados	PZ	Poland
KC	Canada	RC	Cuba
KG	British Guiana	RI	Indonesia
		RM	Roumania
KGB	Gibraltar	S	Sweden
KH	Hong Kong	SA	South Africa
KI	India	SE	Senegal
KJ	Jamaica	SL	El Salvador
KK	Kenya	SR	Union of Soviet Socialist Republics
KR	Rhodesia		
KS	Singapore		
KT	West Indies		
KZ	New Zealand	T	Tunisia
KZA	Zambia	TA	Republic of China (Taiwan)
L	Finland		
LE	Lebanon		
LX	Luxembourg	TH	Thailand
M	Hungary	TK	Turkey
MA	Morocco	U	Uruguay
MG	Madagascar	US	United States of America
MO	Monaco		
MX	Mexico		
MY	Malasia	V	Venezuela
N	Norway	VI	U.S. Virgin I.
NK	Democratic People's Republic of Korea	X	Chile
		Y	Yugoslavia
		Z	Switzerland
OE	Austria		

(*b*) A number, letter, or emblem showing the class to which the yacht belongs.

(*c*) Number of yacht:

A distinguishing number allotted by her own national authority. In the case of a self-administered international class, the number may be allotted by the class owners' association.

Assuming a five-point-meter yacht belonging to the Argentine Republic to be allotted number 3 by the Argentine national authority, her sail shall be marked:

5.5

A3

When there is insufficient space to place the letter or letters showing the yacht's nationality in front of her allotted number, it shall be placed above the number.

(d) The sail numbers, letters, and emblems shall be placed on both sides of the mainsail, at approximately two-thirds of the height of the sail above the boom, so that the lowest number shows when the sail is fully reefed. Sail numbers, letters, and emblems shall sharply contrast in color with the sail and shall be placed at different heights on the two sides of the sail, those on the starboard side being uppermost, to avoid confusion owing to translucency of the sail. The sail numbers only, shall be similarly placed on both sides of the spinnaker, but at approximately half height.

(e) The following sizes for numbers and letters are prescribed:

Size of Numbers and Letters on Sails for the Several Classes Recognized by the I.Y.R.U.

Class	Minimum height of figure and letters		Minimum width occupied by each figure except Figure 1		Minimum thickness of every portion of each figure or letter		Minimum space between adjoining figures	
	Meters.	Ins.	Meters.	Ins.	Meters.	Ins.	Meters.	Ins.
12 Meter	0.66	(26)	0.46	(18)	0.10	(4)	0.15	(6)
13.5 and 15 Meter Cruiser Racer ...	0.66	(26)	0.43	(17)	0.10	(4)	0.15	(6)
10.5 and 12 Meter Cruiser Racer ...	0.56	(22)	0.33	(14)	0.10	(4)	0.12	(5)
9 Meter Cruiser Racer	0.50	(20)	0.33	(13)	0.075	(3)	0.10	(4)
7 and 8 Meter Cruiser Racer ...	0.45	(18)	0.30	(12)	0.075	(3)	0.10	(4)
8 Meter	0.50	(20)	0.36	(14)				
6 Meter .... 5.5 Meter .... 30 sq. Meter ..... 22 sq. Meter ..... Dragon	0.46	(18)	0.30	(12)	0.075	(3)	0.10	(4)
Soling .... "C" Catamaran ... Star .... Tempest	0.38	(15)	0.25	(10)	0.064	(2½)	0.10	(4)
Flying Dutchman ... Tornado Catamaran ..... Australis Catamaran ..... 505 .... 12 sq. Meter Sharpie ...... Lightning .... Finn .... 14 ft. Dinghy	0.30	(12)	0.20	(8)				
Vaurien .... Cadet .... Snipe	0.23	(9)	0.15	(6)				

2.(a) Unless otherwise authorized by the race committee or provided by class rules, a yacht not in one of the classes above shall carry her class number, letter, or emblem and her racing number on her mainsail and spinnaker, as provided above, except that the only size requirement shall be that the numbers, letters, and emblems shall not be less than 10 inches in height for yachts under 22 feet waterline length, not less than 15 inches in height for yachts 22 feet to 32 feet waterline and not less than 18 inches in height for yachts over 32 feet waterline length.

(b) Offshore racing yachts shall carry North American Yacht Racing Union (N.A.Y.R.U.) numbers on mainsails, spinnakers, and all overlapping headsails, effective January 1, 1970.

3. A yacht shall not be disqualified for failing to comply with the provisions of rule 25 without prior warning and adequate opportunity to make correction.

26—Advertisements

A yacht shall not carry any form of advertisement on her hull or equipment, except that:

(a) Not more than one sailmaker's mark, if any, shall be placed on each side of the sail, not more than 15 per cent of the length of its foot from the tack, and

(b) builders' marks may be placed on the hull, spars, or equipment.

Such marks (or plates) shall fit within a square not exceeding 15×15 cms. (6×6 ins.).

27—Forestays and Jib Tacks

Unless otherwise prescribed in the class rules, forestays and jib tacks (not including spinnaker staysails when not close-hauled) shall be fixed approximately in the centerline of the yacht.

28—Flags

A yacht may display her private signal on the leach of her mainsail or from her mizzen mast head, and a wind indicator of a solid color or a feather. Other flags shall not be displayed except for signaling. A yacht shall not be disqualified for failing to comply with the provisions of this rule without warning and adequate opportunity to make correction.

(Numbers 29 and 30 are spare numbers.)

PART IV

SAILING RULES WHEN YACHTS MEET

Helmsman's Rights and Obligations Concerning Right of Way

The rules of Part IV apply only between yachts which either are intending to race *or are* racing *in the same or different races, and, except when rule 3.2(b)(ii) applies, replace the International Regulations for Preventing Collisions at Sea or Government Right-of-Way Rules applicable to the area concerned, from the time a yacht intending to* race *begins to sail about in the vicinity of the starting line until she has either* finished *or retired and has left the vicinity of the course.*

SECTION A—RULES WHICH ALWAYS APPLY

31—Disqualification

1. A yacht may be disqualified for infringing a rule of Part IV only when the infringement occurs while she is racing, whether or not a collision results.

2. A yacht may be disqualified before or after she is racing for seriously hindering a yacht which is racing, or for infringing the sailing instructions.

32—Avoiding Collisions

A right-of-way yacht which makes no attempt to avoid a collision resulting in serious damage may be disqualified as well as the other yacht.

33—Retiring from Race

A yacht which realizes she has infringed a racing rule or a sailing instruction should retire promptly; but, when she persists in racing, other yachts shall continue to accord her such rights as she may have under the rules of Part IV.

34—Limitations on the Right-of-Way Yacht to Alter Course

When one yacht is required to keep clear of another, the right-of-way yacht shall not (except to the extent permitted by rule 38.1, Right-of-way Yacht Luffing after Starting), so alter course as to prevent the other yacht from keeping clear; or to obstruct her while so doing.

35—Hailing

A right-of-way yacht, except when luffing under rule 38.1, Luffing after Starting, should hail before or when making an alteration of course which may not be foreseen by the other yacht or when claiming the establishment or termination of an overlap at a mark or obstruction.

SECTION B—OPPOSITE TACK RULE

36—Fundamental Rule

A port-tack yacht shall keep clear of a starboard-tack yacht.

SECTION C—SAME TACK RULES

37—Fundamental Rules

1. A windward yacht shall keep clear of a leeward yacht.

2. A yacht clear astern shall keep clear of a yacht clear ahead.

3. A yacht which establishes an overlap to leeward from clear astern shall allow the windward yacht ample room and opportunity to keep clear, and during the existence of that overlap the leeward yacht shall not sail above her proper course.

38—Right-of-Way Yacht Luffing after Starting

1. **Luffing Rights and Limitations.** After she has started and cleared the starting line, a yacht clear ahead or a leeward yacht may luff as she pleases, except that:

A leeward yacht shall not sail above her proper course while an overlap exists if, at any time during its existence, the helmsman of the windward yacht (when sighting abeam from his normal station and sailing no higher than the leeward yacht) has been abreast or forward of the mainmast of the leeward yacht.

2. **Overlap Limitations.** For the purpose of this rule: An overlap does not exist unless the yachts are clearly within two overall lengths of the longer yacht; and an overlap which exists between two yachts when the leading yacht starts, or when one or both of them completes a tack or jibe, shall be regarded as a new overlap beginning at that time.

3. **Hailing to Stop or Prevent a Luff.** When there is doubt, the leeward yacht may assume that she has the right to luff unless the helmsman of the windward yacht has hailed "Mast Abeam," or words to that effect. The leeward yacht shall be governed by such hail, and, if she deems it improper, her only remedy is to protest.

4. **Curtailing a Luff.** The windward yacht shall not cause a luff to be curtailed because of her proximity to the leeward yacht unless an obstruction, a third yacht or other object restricts her ability to respond.

5. **Luffing Two or More Yachts.** A yacht shall not luff unless she has the right to luff all yachts which would be affected by her luff, in which case they shall all respond even if an intervening yacht or yachts would not otherwise have the right to luff.

39—Sailing Below a Proper Course

A yacht which is on a free leg of the course shall not sail below her proper course when she is clearly within three of her overall lengths of either a leeward yacht or a yacht clear astern which is steering a course to pass to leeward.

40—Right-of-Way Luffing before Starting

Before a yacht has started and cleared the starting line, any luff on her part which causes another yacht to have to alter course to avoid a collision shall be carried out slowly and in such a way so as to give the windward yacht room and opportunity to keep clear, but before her starting signal, the leeward yacht shall not so luff above a close-hauled course, unless the helmsman of the windward yacht (sighting abeam from his normal station) is abaft the mainmast of the leeward yacht. Rules 38.3, Hailing to Stop or Prevent a

Luff; 38.4, Curtailing a Luff; and 38.5, Luffing Two or More Yachts, also apply.

SECTION D—CHANGING TACK RULES

41—Tacking or Jibing

1. A yacht which is either tacking or jibing shall keep clear of a yacht on a tack.

2. A yacht shall neither tack nor jibe into a position which will give her right of way unless she does so far enough from a yacht on a tack to enable this yacht to keep clear without having to begin to alter her course until after the tack or jibe has been completed.

3. A yacht which tacks or jibes has the onus of satisfying the race committee that she completed her tack or jibe in accordance with rule 41.2.

4. When two yachts are both tacking or both jibing at the same time, the one on the other's port side shall keep clear.

SECTION E—RULES OF EXCEPTION AND SPECIAL APPLICATION

When a rule of this section applies, to the extent to which it explicitly provides rights and obligations, it overrides any conflicting rule of Part IV which precedes it except the rules of Section A—Rules Which Always Apply.

42—Rounding or Passing Marks and Obstructions

When yachts either on the same tack or, after starting and clearing the starting line, on opposite tacks, are about to round or pass a mark on the same required side or an obstruction on the same side:

When Overlapped

1.(*a*) An outside yacht shall give each yacht overlapping her on the inside, room to round or pass it, except as provided in rules 42.1(c), (d), and (e). Room includes room to tack or jibe when either is an integral part of the rounding or passing maneuver.

(*b*) When an inside yacht of two or more overlapped yachts on opposite tacks will have to jibe in rounding a mark in order most directly to assume a proper course to the next mark, she shall jibe at the first reasonable opportunity.

(c) When two yachts on opposite tacks are on a beat or when one of them will have to tack either to round the mark or to avoid the obstruction, as between each other rule 42.1(a) shall not apply and they are subject to rules 36, Opposite Tack Fundamental Rule, and 41, Tacking or Jibing.

(d) An outside leeward yacht with luffing rights may take an inside yacht to windward of a mark provided that she hails to that effect and begins to luff before she is within two of her overall lengths of the mark and provided that she also passes to windward of it.

(e) When approaching the starting line to start, a leeward yacht shall be under no obligation to give any windward yacht room to pass to leeward of a starting mark surrounded by navigable water; but, after the starting signal, a leeward yacht shall not deprive a windward yacht of room at such a mark by sailing either above the first mark or above close-hauled.

When Clear Astern and Clear Ahead

2.(a) A yacht clear astern shall keep clear in anticipation of and during the rounding or passing maneuver when the yacht clear ahead remains on the same tack or jibes.

(b) A yacht clear ahead which tacks to round a mark is subject to rule 41, Tacking or Jibing, but a yacht clear astern shall not luff above close-hauled so as to prevent the yacht clear ahead from tacking.

Restrictions on Establishing and Maintaining an Overlap

3.(a) A yacht clear astern shall not establish an inside overlap and be entitled to room under rule 42.1(a) when the yacht clear ahead:

(i) is within two of her overall lengths of the mark or obstruction, except as provided in rules 42.3(b) and 42.3(c); or

(ii) is unable to give the required room.

(b) The two lengths determinative of rule 42.3(a)(i) shall not apply to yachts, of which one has tacked in the vicinity of a mark, unless when the tack is completed the yachts are clearly more than two overall lengths from the mark.

(c) A yacht clear astern may establish an overlap between the yacht clear ahead and a continuing obstruction such as a shoal or the shore, only when there is room for her to do so in safety.

(d) (i) A yacht clear ahead shall be under no obligation to give room to a yacht clear astern before an overlap is established.

(ii) A yacht which claims an inside overlap has the onus of satisfying the race committee that the overlap was established in proper time.

(e) (i) When an outside yacht is overlapped at the time she comes within two of her overall lengths of a mark, she shall continue to be bound by rule 42.1(a) to give room as required even though the overlap may thereafter be broken.

(ii) An outside yacht which claims to have broken an overlap has the onus of satisfying the race committee that she became clear ahead when she was more than two of her overall lengths from the mark.

43—Close-hauled, Hailing for Room to Tack at Obstructions

1. **Hailing.** When two close-hauled yachts are on the same tack and safe pilotage requires the yacht clear ahead or the leeward yacht to make a substantial alteration of course to clear an obstruction, and if she intends to tack, but cannot tack without colliding with the other yacht, she shall hail the other yacht for room to tack, but she shall not hail and tack simultaneously.

2. **Responding.** The hailed yacht at the earliest possible moment after the hail shall either:

(*a*) tack, in which case, the hailing yacht shall begin to tack either:

(i) before the hailed yacht has completed her tack, or

(ii) if she cannot then tack without colliding with the hailed yacht, immediately she is able to tack, or

(*b*) reply "You tack," or words to that effect, if in her opinion she can keep clear without tacking or after postponing her tack. In this case:

(i) the hailing yacht shall immediately tack and

(ii) the hailed yacht shall keep clear.

(iii) The onus shall lie on the hailed yacht which replied "You tack" to satisfy the race committee that she kept clear.

3. **Limitation on Right to Room**

(*a*) When the obstruction is a mark which the hailed yacht can fetch, the hailing yacht shall not be entitled to room to tack and the hailed yacht shall immediately so inform the hailing yacht.

(*b*) If, thereafter, the hailing yacht again hails for room to tack, she shall, after receiving it, retire immediately.

(*c*) If, after having refused to respond to a hail under rule 43.3(a), the hailed yacht fails to fetch, she shall retire immediately.

44—Yachts Returning to Start

1.(*a*) A premature starter when returning to start, or a yacht working into position from the wrong side of the starting line or its extensions, when the starting signal is made, shall keep clear of all yachts which are starting, or have started, correctly, until she is wholly on the right side of the starting line or its extensions.

(*b*) Thereafter, she shall be accorded the rights under the rules of Part IV of a yacht which is starting correctly; but if she thereby acquires right of way over another yacht which is starting correctly, she shall allow that yacht ample room and opportunity to keep clear.

2. A premature starter while continuing to sail the course and until it is obvious that she is returning to start, shall be accorded the rights under the rules of Part IV of a yacht which has started.

45—Yachts Rerounding after Touching a Mark

1. A yacht which has touched a mark and is about to correct her error in accordance with rule 52.1, Touching a Mark, shall keep clear of all other yachts which are about to round or pass it or have rounded or passed it correctly, until she has rounded it completely and has cleared it and is on a proper course to the next mark.

2. A yacht which has touched a mark, while continuing to sail the course and until it is obvious that she is returning to round it completely in accordance with rule 52.1, Touching a Mark, shall be accorded rights under the rules of Part IV.

SECTION F—WHEN NOT UNDER WAY

46—Anchored, Aground, or Capsized

1. A yacht under way shall keep clear of another yacht racing which is anchored, aground, or capsized. Of two anchored yachts, the one which anchored later shall keep clear, except that a yacht which is dragging shall keep clear of one which is not.

2. A yacht anchored or aground shall indicate the fact to any yacht which may be in danger of fouling her. Unless the size of the yachts or the weather conditions make some other signal necessary a hail is sufficient indication.

3. A yacht shall not be penalized for fouling a yacht in distress which she is attempting to assist or a yacht which goes aground or capsizes immediately ahead of her.

(Numbers 47 and 48 are spare numbers.)

PART V

OTHER SAILING RULES

Obligations of Helmsman and Crew in Handling a Yacht

Except for rule 49, a yacht is subject to the rules of Part V only while she is racing.

49—Fair Sailing

A yacht shall attempt to win a race only by fair sailing, superior speed and skill, and, except in team races, by individual effort. However, a yacht may be disqualified under this rule only in the case of a clear-cut violation of the above principles and only if no other rule applies.

50—Ranking as a Starter

A yacht which sails about in the vicinity of the starting line between her preparatory and starting signals shall rank as a starter, even if she does not start.

51—Sailing the Course

1.(*a*) A yacht shall start and finish only as prescribed in the starting and finishing definitions, even if the committee boat is anchored on the side of the starting or finishing mark opposite to that prescribed in the sailing instructions.

(*b*) Unless otherwise prescribed in the sailing instructions, a yacht which either crosses prematurely, or is on the wrong side of the starting line, or its extensions, at the starting signal, shall return and start in accordance with the definition.

(*c*) Unless otherwise prescribed in the sailing instructions, when after a general recall, any part of a yacht's hull, crew, or equipment is over the starting line during the minute before her starting signal, she shall thereafter pass on the course side of and around one of the starting marks and cross the starting line in the direction of the first mark.

(*d*) Failure of a yacht to see or hear her recall notification shall not relieve her of her obligation to start correctly.

2. A yacht shall sail the course so as to round or pass each mark on the required side in correct sequence, and so that a string representing her wake from the time she starts until she finishes would, when drawn taut, lie on the required side of each mark.

3. A mark has a required side for a yacht as long as she is on a leg which it begins, bounds, or ends. A starting mark begins to have a required side for a yacht when she starts. A finishing mark ceases to have a required side for a yacht as soon as she finishes.

4. A yacht which rounds or passes a mark on the wrong side may correct her error by making her course conform to the requirements of rule 51.2.

5. It is not necessary for a yacht to cross the finishing line completely. After finishing she may clear it in either direction.

6. In the absence of the race committee, a yacht shall take her own time when she finishes, and report the time taken to the race committee as soon as possible. If there is no longer an established finishing line, the finishing line shall be a line extending from the required side of the finishing mark at right angles to the last leg of the course, and 100 yards long or as much longer as may be necessary to insure adequate depth of water in crossing it.

52—Touching a Mark

1. A yacht which either:

(*a*) touches:

    (i) a starting mark before starting:

    (ii) a mark which begins, bounds or ends the leg of the course on which she is sailing: or

    (iii) a finishing mark after finishing, or

(*b*) causes a mark vessel to shift to avoid being touched,

shall retire immediately, unless she claims that she was wrongfully compelled to touch it by another yacht, in which case she shall protest. However, unless otherwise prescribed in the sailing instructions, when the mark is surrounded by navigable water, a yacht may correct her error by making one complete rounding of the mark, leaving it on the required side without touching it, in addition to rounding or passing it as required to sail the course. In the case of a mark at the starboard end of the starting or finishing line, such complete rounding shall be clockwise, and at the port end of a starting or finishing line anti-clockwise.

2. For the purposes of rule 52.1: Every ordinary part of a mark ranks as part of it, including a flag, flagpole, boom, or hoisted boat, but excluding ground tackle and any object either accidentally or temporarily attached to it.

53—Fog Signals and Lights

1. Every yacht shall observe the International Regulations for Preventing Collisions at Sea or Government Rules for fog signals and, as a minimum, the carrying of lights at night.

2. The use of additional special purpose lights such as masthead, spreader, or jib luff lights shall not constitute grounds for protest.

54—Setting and Sheeting Sails

1. **Changing Sails.** While changing headsails and spinnakers a replacing sail may be fully set and trimmed before the sail it replaces is taken in, but only one mainsail and, except when changing, only one spinnaker shall be carried set.

2. **Sheeting Sails to Spars.** Unless otherwise prescribed by the class rules, any sail may be sheeted to or led above a boom regularly used for a working sail and permanently attached to the mast to which the head of the working sail is set, but no sails shall be sheeted over or through outriggers. An outrigger is any fitting so placed, except as permitted in the first sentence of rule 54.2, that it could exert outward pressure on a sheet at a point from which, with the yacht upright, a vertical line would fall outside the hull or deck planking at that point, or outside such other position as class rules prescribe. For the purpose of this rule: Bulwarks, rails, and rubbing strakes are not part of the hull or deck planking. A boom of a boomed foresail which requires no adjustment when tacking is not an outrigger.

3. **Spinnaker, Spinnaker Pole.** A spinnaker shall not be set without a pole. The tack of a spinnaker when set and drawing shall be in close proximity to the outboard end of a spinnaker pole. Any headsail may be attached to a spinnaker pole provided a spinnaker is not set. A sail tacked down abaft the foremost mast is not a headsail. Only one spinnaker pole shall be used at a time and when in use shall be carried only on the side of the foremost mast opposite to the main boom and shall be fixed to the mast. Rule 54.3 shall not apply when shifting a spinnaker pole or sail attached thereto.

55—Owner Steering Another Yacht

An owner shall not steer any yacht other than his own in a race wherein his own yacht competes, without the previous consent of the race committee.

55A—Paid Hand Steering

A paid hand shall not steer a yacht of less than 32 feet waterline length.

56—Boarding

Unless otherwise prescribed in the sailing instructions, no person shall board a yacht except for the purpose of rule 58, Rendering Assistance, or to attend an injured or ill member of the crew or temporarily as one of the crew of a vessel fouled.

57—Leaving, Man Overboard

Unless otherwise prescribed in the sailing instructions, no person on board a yacht when her preparatory signal was made shall leave, unless injured or ill, or for the purposes of rule 58, Rendering Assistance, except that any member of the crew may fall overboard or leave her to swim, stand on the bottom as a means of anchoring, haul her out ashore to effect repairs, reef sails or bail out, or help her to get clear after grounding or fouling another vessel or object, provided that this person is back on board before the yacht continues in the race.

58—Rendering Assistance

Every yacht shall render all possible assistance to any vessel or person in peril, when in a position to do so.

59—Outside Assistance

Except as permitted by rules 56, Boarding, 58, Rendering Assistance, and 64, Aground or Foul of an Obstruction, a yacht shall neither receive outside assistance nor use any gear other than that on board when her preparatory signal was made.

60—Means of Propulsion

A yacht shall be propelled only by the natural action of the wind on the sails, spars and hull, and water on the hull, and shall not pump, "ooch" or rock, as described in Appendix 2, nor check way by abnormal means, except for the purpose of rule 58, Rendering Assistance, or of recovering a man who has accidentally fallen overboard. An oar, paddle, or other object may be used in emergency for steering. An anchor may be sent out in a boat only as permitted by rule 64, Aground or Foul of an Obstruction.

61—Sounding

Any means of sounding may be used provided rule 60, Means of Propulsion, is not infringed.

62—Manual Power

A yacht shall use manual power only, except that a power winch or windlass may be used in weighing anchor or in getting clear after running aground or fouling any object, and a power bilge pump may be used in an auxiliary yacht.

63—Anchoring and Making Fast

1. A yacht may anchor. Means of anchoring may include the crew standing on the bottom and any weight lowered to the bottom. A yacht shall recover any anchor or weight used, and any chain or rope attached to it, before continuing in the race, unless after making every effort she finds recovery impossible. In this case she shall report the circumstances to the race committee, which may disqualify her if it considers the loss due either to inadequate gear or to insufficient effort to recover it.

2. A yacht shall be afloat and off moorings, before her preparatory signal, but may be anchored, and shall not thereafter make fast or be made fast by means other than anchoring, nor be hauled out, except for the purpose of rule 64, Aground or Foul of an Obstruction, or to effect repairs, reef sails, or bail out.

64—Aground or Foul of an Obstruction

A yacht, after grounding or fouling another vessel or other object, is subject to rule 62, Manual Power, and may, in getting clear, use her own anchors, boats, ropes, spars, and other gear; may send out an anchor in a boat; may be refloated by her crew going overboard either to stand on the bottom or to go ashore to push off; but may receive outside assistance only from the crew of the vessel fouled. A yacht shall recover all her own gear used in getting clear before continuing in the race.

65—Skin Friction

A yacht shall not eject or release from a container any substance (such as polymer) the purpose of which is, or could be, to reduce the frictional resistance of the hull by altering the character of the flow of water inside the boundary layer.

66—Increasing Stability

Unless otherwise prescribed by her class rules or in the sailing instructions, a yacht shall not use any device, such as a trapeze or plank, to project outboard the weight of any of the crew, nor, when a yacht is equipped with lifelines, shall any member of the crew station any part of his torso outside them, other than temporarily.

(Number 67 is a spare number.)

PART VI

PROTESTS, DISQUALIFICATIONS AND APPEALS

68—Protests

1. A yacht can protest against any other yacht, except that a protest for an alleged infringement of the rules of Part IV can be made only by a yacht directly involved in, or witnessing an incident.

2. A protest occurring between yachts competing in separate races sponsored by different clubs shall be heard by a combined committee of both clubs.

3.(a) A protest for an infringement of the rules or sailing instructions occurring during a race shall be signified by showing a flag (International Code flag "B" is always acceptable, irrespective of any other provisions in the sailing instructions) conspicuously in the rigging of the protesting yacht at the first reasonable opportunity and keeping it flying until she has finished or retired, or if the first reasonable opportunity occurs after finishing, until acknowledged by the race committee. In the case of a yacht sailed single-handed, it will be sufficient if the flag (whether displayed in the rigging or not) is brought to the notice of the yacht protested against as soon as possible after the incident and to the race committee when the protesting yacht finishes.

(b) A yacht which has no knowledge of the facts justifying a protest until after she has finished or retired may nevertheless protest without having shown a protest flag.

(c) A protesting yacht shall try to inform the yacht protested against that a protest will be lodged.

(d) Such a protest shall be in writing and signed by the owner or his representative, and should state:

(i) The date, time, and whereabout of the incident.

(ii) The particular rule or rules or sailing instructions alleged to have been infringed.

(iii) A statement of the facts.

(iv) Unless irrelevant, a diagram of the incident.

(e) Unless otherwise prescribed in the sailing instructions a protesting yacht shall deliver, or if that is not possible, mail her protest to the race committee:

(i) within two hours of the time she finishes the race, or within such time as may have been prescribed in the sailing instructions under rule 3.2(b)(xiv), unless the race committee should have reason to extend these time limits, or

(ii) should she not finish the race, within such a time as the race committee may consider reasonable in the circumstances of the case.

A protest shall be accompanied by such fee, if any, as may have been prescribed in the sailing instructions under rule 3.2(b)(xiv).

(f) The race committee shall allow any omissions in the details required by rule 68.3 (d) to be remedied at a later time.

4.(a) A protest that a measurement, scantling, or flotation rule has been infringed while racing, or that a classification or rating certificate is for any reason invalid, shall be lodged with the race committee not later than 6 P.M. on the day following the race. The race committee shall send a copy of the protest to the yacht protested against and, should there appear to be reasonable grounds for the protest, it shall refer the question to an authority qualified to decide such questions.

(b) The race committee, in making its decision, shall be governed by the determination of such authority. Copies of such decision shall be sent to all yachts involved.

5.(a) A yacht which claims that her chances of winning a prize have been prejudiced by an action or omission of the race committee, may seek redress from the race committee in accordance with the requirements for a protest provided in rules 68.3(d), (e) and (f).

(b) When the race committee decides that such action or omission was prejudicial, and that the result of the race was altered thereby, it shall cancel or abandon the race, or make such other arrangement as it deems equitable.

6. A protest made in writing shall not be withdrawn, but shall be decided by the race com-

mittee, unless prior to the hearing full responsibility is acknowledged by one or more yachts.

69—Refusal of a Protest

1. When the race committee decides that a protest does not conform to the requirements of rule 68, Protests, it shall inform the protesting yacht that her protest will not be heard and of the reasons for such decision.

2. Such a decision shall not be reached without giving the protesting yacht all opportunity of bringing evidence that the requirements of rule 68, Protests, were complied with.

70—Hearings

1. When the race committee decides that a protest conforms to all the requirements of rule 68, Protests, it shall call a hearing as soon as possible. The protest, or a copy of it, shall be made available to all yachts involved, and each shall be notified, in writing if practicable, of the time and place set for the hearing. A reasonable time shall be allowed for the preparation of defense. At the hearing, the race committee shall take the evidence presented by the parties to the protest and such other evidence as it may consider necessary. The parties to the protest, or a representative of each, shall have the right to be present, but all others, except one witness at a time while testifying, may be excluded. A yacht other than one named in the protest, which is involved in that protest, shall have all the privileges of yachts originally named in it.

2. A yacht shall not be penalized without a hearing, except as provided in rule 73.1(a), Disqualification without Protest.

3. Failure on the part of any of the interested parties or a representative to make an effort to attend the hearing of the protest may justify the race committee in deciding the protest as it thinks fit without a full hearing.

71—Decisions

The race committee shall make its decision promptly after the hearing. Each decision shall be communicated to the parties involved, and shall state fully the facts and grounds on which it is based and shall specify the rules, if any, infringed. If requested by any of the parties, such decision shall be given in writing and shall include the race committee's diagram. The findings of the race committee as to the facts involved shall be final.

72—Disqualification after Protest

1. When the race committee, after hearing a protest or acting under rule 73, Disqualification without Protest, or any appeal authority, is satisfied:

    (a) that a yacht has infringed any of these rules or the sailing instructions, or

    (b) that in consequence of her neglect of any of these rules or the sailing instructions she has compelled other yachts to infringe any of these rules or the sailing instructions,

she shall be disqualified unless the sailing instructions applicable to that race provide some other penalty. Such disqualification or other penalty shall be imposed, irrespective of whether the rule or sailing instruction which led to the disqualification or penalty was mentioned in the protest, or the yacht which was at fault was mentioned or protested against, e.g., the protesting yacht or a third yacht might be disqualified and the protested yacht absolved.

2. For the purpose of awarding points in a series, a retirement after an infringement of any of these rules or the sailing instructions shall not rank as a disqualification. This penalty can be imposed only in accordance with rules 72, Disqualification after Protest, and 73, Disqualification without Protest.

3. When a yacht either is disqualified or has retired, the next in order shall be awarded her place.

73—Disqualification without Protest

1.(a) A yacht which fails either to start or to finish may be disqualified without protest or hearing, after the conclusion of the race, except that she shall be entitled to a hearing, provided she satisfies the race committee that an error may have been made.

    (*b*) A yacht so penalized shall be informed of the action taken, either by letter or by notification in the racing results.

2. When the race committee:

    (*a*) sees an apparent infringement by a yacht of any of these rules or the sailing instructions (except as provided in rule 73.1), or

    (*b*) receives a report not later than the same day from a witness who was neither competing in the race, nor otherwise an interested party, alleging such an infringement, or

    (*c*) has reasonable grounds for supposing from the evidence at the hearing of a valid protest, that any yacht involved in the incident may have committed such an infringement,

it may notify such yacht thereof orally, or if that is not possible, in writing, delivered or mailed not later than one day after:

    (i) the finish of the race, or

    (ii) the receipt of the report, or

    (iii) the hearing of the protest.

Such notice shall contain a statement of the pertinent facts and of the particular rule or rules or sailing instructions believed to have been infringed, and the race committee shall act thereon in the same manner as if it had been a protest made by a competitor.

74—Penalties for Gross Infringement of Rules

1. When a gross infringement of any of these rules or the sailing instructions is proved against the owner, the owner's representative, the helmsman, or sailing master of a yacht, such persons may be disqualified by the national authority, for any period it may think fit, from either steering or sailing in a yacht in any race held under its jurisdiction.

2. Notice of any penalty adjudged under this rule shall be communicated to the I.Y.R.U. which shall inform all national authorities.

75—Persons Interested Not to Take Part in Decision

No member of either a race committee or of any appeals authority shall take part in the discussion or decision upon any disputed question in which he is an interested party, but this does not preclude him from giving evidence in such a case.

76—Expenses Incurred by Protest

Unless otherwise prescribed by the race committee, the fees and expenses entailed by a protest or measurement or classification shall be paid by the unsuccessful party.

77—Appeals

1. LIMITATIONS ON RIGHT TO APPEAL—Appeals involving solely the interpretation of the racing rules may be taken to the Appeals Committee of the Union for final determination:

    a. if the club is a member of the Union but is not a member of a local association belonging to the Union, by an owner or his representative from a decision of the race committee;

    b. if the club is a member of a local association belonging to the Union, by an owner or his representative or by the race committee from a decision of the local association.

2. PREPARATION OF APPEAL PAPERS—All appeals shall be in writing and shall set forth the grounds of the appeal and be signed by the appellant. They shall be filed with the Secretary of the Union by the body rendering the decision appealed from, within thirty days after the decision is announced, together with—

    (*a*) a copy of the sailing instructions;

    (*b*) a copy of the protest or request for redress;

    (*c*) the names of the yachts represented at the hearing, and of any yacht duly notified of the hearing, but not represented, and the name and address of the representative of each of said yachts;

    (*d*) a copy of the decision of the race committee containing a full statement of the facts found by it;

(*e*) an official diagram prepared by the race committee in accordance with the facts found by it and signed by it and showing, (i) the course to the next mark or, if close by, the mark itself and its required side, (ii) the direction and velocity of the wind, (iii) the set of the current, if any, and (iv) the position or positions and tracks of the yachts involved;

(*f*) a copy of the decision, if any, of the local association.

3. DECISION OF APPEALS COMMITTEE—Decisions of the appeals committee shall be in writing and the grounds of each decision shall be specified therein. Each decision shall be filed with the Secretary of the Union, who shall send copies thereof to all parties to the infringement and appeal.

TEAM RACING RULES

Team racing shall be sailed under the yacht racing rules of the International Yacht Racing Union as adopted by the North American Yacht Racing Union supplemented as follows:

SAILING RULES

1. A yacht may maneuver against a yacht sailing another leg of the course only if she can do so while sailing a proper course relative to the leg which she herself is sailing.

2. Except to protect her own or a teammate's finishing position, a yacht in one team which is completing the last leg of the course shall not maneuver against a yacht in another team which has no opponent astern of her.

3. Right of way may be waived by teammates, provided that by so doing an opponent is not baulked; but the benefits of rule 12, Yacht Materially Prejudiced, shall not be available to a yacht damaged by contact between teammates.

4. When two overlapping yachts on the same tack are in the act of rounding or passing on the required side of a mark at which their proper course changes:

(a) If the leeward yacht is inside, she may, if she has luffing rights hold her course or luff. If she does not have luffing rights, she shall promptly assume her proper course to the next mark whether or not she has to jibe:

(b) If the windward yacht is inside, she shall promptly luff up to her proper course to the next mark, or if she cannot assume such proper course without tacking and does not choose to tack, she shall promptly luff up to close-hauled. This clause does not restrict a leeward yacht's right to luff under rule 38, Luffing after Starting.

SCORING

5. **Each Race**

(a) Yachts shall score three-quarters of a point for first place, two points for second place, three points for third place, and so on.

(b) A yacht which infringes any rule and retires with reasonable promptness shall score one point more than the number of yachts in the race, but if her retirement is tardy, or if she fails to retire and is subsequently disqualified, she shall score four points more than the number of yachts in the race.

(c) A yacht which infringes a rule shortly before or when finishing shall be considered to have retired with reasonable promptness if she notifies the race committee of her retirement as soon as is reasonably practicable.

(d) A yacht which does not finish for a reason other than an infringement shall score points equal to the number of starters in the race, except as provided in (e)

(e) After all the yachts of one team have finished or retired, the race committee may stop the race and allot to each yacht of the other team which is still racing and underway the points she would have received had she finished.

(f) The team with the lowest total point score shall be the winner of the race.

6. The Series

(a) When only two teams are competing, the team winning the greater number of races sailed shall be the winner of the series.

(b) When three or more teams are competing in a series consisting of races each of which is between two teams, the team winning the greatest number of races shall be the winner.

(c) When three or more teams are all competing in each race the team with the lowest total point score in all races sailed shall be the winner.

7. Breaking Ties

(a) When two or more teams are tied because of each having won the same number of races, if practicable the tie should be resolved by a sail off.

(b) If there is a tie when more than two teams are competing, the team which has beaten the other tied team or teams in the most races shall be the winner. Failing this, the team with the lowest point score in all races sailed shall be the winner. When teams tie with only two teams competing and a sail off is impracticable, the tie shall be broken in favor of the winner of the last race.

ADDENDUM

RULES RECOMMENDED TO APPLY WHEN THE HOME TEAM FURNISHES ALL RACING YACHTS

A. ASSIGNMENT OF YACHTS: The home team shall furnish the visiting team with a list of the yachts to be used and of the sail numbers assigned to each yacht for the match. The home team shall divide these yachts into as many equal groups as there are competing teams and these groups shall be drawn for by lot for the first race. Skipper assignment to the yachts shall then be made as each team decides for itself, except that a skipper shall not at any time sail his own yacht. The groups of yachts shall be exchanged between races so that, as far as possible, each group will be sailed in turn by each team. In a two-team match after an even number of races, if either team requests that the yachts be regrouped, the home team shall redivide them into new groups which shall be drawn for by lot; except that for the final odd race of a two-team match, the visiting team may select the group it wishes to sail.

B. ASSIGNMENT OF SAILS: If sails as well as yachts are furnished by the home team, the sails used by each yacht in the first race shall be used by her throughout the series and the substitution of a spare or extra sail shall not be permitted unless because of damage or for some other valid reason, a change is approved by the jury or judges after notification to both teams.

C. GROUP IDENTIFICATION: One group shall carry no marking. The second group shall carry dark colored strips or pennants, and additional groups shall carry light or differently colored strips or pennants. Strips or pennants should usually be furnished by the home team and should be attached to the same conspicuous place on each boat of a group, such as the after end of the main boom or permanent backstay.

D. BREAKDOWNS: When a breakdown results in substantial loss, the jury or judges shall decide whether or not it was the fault of the crew. In general, a breakdown caused by defective equipment, or the result of a foul by an opponent shall not be deemed the fault of the crew, and a breakdown caused by careless handling or capsizing shall be. In case of doubt, the doubt shall be resolved in favor of the crew.

E. If the jury or judges decide that the breakdown was not the fault of the crew and that a reasonably competent crew could not have remedied the defect in time to prevent substantial loss, they shall cancel the race, or order it to be resailed, or award the breakdown yacht the number of points she would have received had she finished in the same position in the race she held when she broke down. In case of doubt as to her position when she broke down, the doubt shall be resolved against her.

F. SPARES: The home team shall be prepared to furnish one or more extra yachts and sails to replace any which, in the opinion of the jury or judges, are unfit for use in the remaining races.

APPENDIX I

Amateur

1. For the purpose of international yacht races in which yachts entering are required to have one or more amateurs on board, and in other races with similar requirements, an amateur is a yachtsman who engages in yacht racing as a pastime as distinguished from a means of obtaining a livelihood. No yachtsman shall lose amateur status by reason of the fact that his livelihood is derived from designing or constructing any boats or parts of boats, or accessories of boats, or sails or from other professions associated with the sea and ships.

2. Any yachtsman whose amateur status is questioned or is in doubt, may apply to the national authority of the country of his residence for recognition of his amateur status. Any such applicant may be required to provide such particulars and evidence and to pay such fee as the national authority may prescribe. Recognition may be suspended or cancelled by the national authority by which it was granted.

3. The permanent committee of the International Yacht Racing Union, or any tribunal nominated by the chairman of that committee, may review the decision of any authority as to the amateur status of a yachtsman for the purpose of competing in international races.

4. For the purposes of participation in the Olympic Games an amateur is required to conform to the eligibility rules of the International Olympic Committee. Information on these eligibility requirements is available from all national authorities.

APPENDIX II

"Pumping" Sails, "Ooching," and "Rocking"

"Pumping" consists of frequent rapid trimming of sails with no particular reference to a change in true or apparent wind direction. To promote planing or surfing, rapid trimming of sails need not be considered "pumping."

The purpose of this interpretation of rule 60 is to prevent "fanning" one's boat around the course by flapping the sail similar to a bird's wing in flight. "Pumping" or frequent, quickly repeated trimming and releasing of the mainsail to increase propulsion is not allowed and is not "the natural action of the wind on the sails."

Where surfing or planing conditions exist, however, rule 60 allows taking advantage of "the natural action of water on the hull" through the rapid trimming of sails and adjustment of helm to promote (initiate) surfing or planing.

The test is whether or not the conditions are such that by rapid trimming of sails a boat could be started surfing or planing. A skipper challenged for "pumping" will have to prove, through the performance either of his own boat or of other boats, that surfing or planing conditions existed, and that the frequency of his rapid trimming was geared to the irregular or cyclical wave forms rather than to a regular rhythmic pattern.

Note that the interpretation refers to "promoting" and not to "maintaining" surfing or planing. Once a boat has started surfing or planing on a particular set of wave forms, from then on she must let the natural action of wind and water propel her without further rapid trimming and releasing of the sails.

Rapid trimming when approaching marks or the finishing line or other critical points should be consistent with that which was practiced throughout the leg.

"Ooching," which consists of lunging forward

and stopping abruptly, falls in the same category as "pumping."

"Rocking" consists of persistently rolling a yacht from side to side.

APPENDIX III

INTERNATIONAL YACHT RACING UNION RULES BEFORE CHANGES PRESCRIBED BY THE N.A.Y.R.U.

(For use only when racing outside of the jurisdiction of the N.A.Y.R.U.)

4—Signals

1. **International Code Flag Signals**

"AP"—Answering Pennant—Postponement Signal.

When displayed alone over a class signal, means:

"The scheduled time of the start of the designated race is postponed 15 minutes."

(This postponement can be extended indefinitely in 15-minute intervals by dipping and rehoisting the signal.)

When displayed over 1 ball or shape over a class signal, means:

"The scheduled time of the start of the designated race is postponed 30 minutes."

(This postponement can be extended indefinitely by the addition of 1 ball or shape for every 15 minutes.)

When displayed over one of the numeral pennants 1 to 9 over a class signal, means:

"The scheduled time of the start of the designated race is postponed 1 hour, 2 hours, etc."

When displayed over the letter "A" over a class signal, means:

"The designated race is postponed to a later date."

When any of the above signals is displayed without a class signal below, means:

"The whole sailing programme is postponed in accordance with the signal made."

8—Recalls

1. Unless otherwise prescribed by the national authority or in the sailing instructions, the race committee may allot a recall number or letter to each yacht, in accordance with rule 3.2(b)(viii), using yachts' sail numbers or letters when practicable.

18—Entries

Unless otherwise prescribed by the national authority or by the race committee in either the notice or the sailing instructions, entries shall be made in the following form:

FORM OF ENTRY

To the Secretary . . . . *Club*
   Please enter the yacht . . . . *for*
the . . . . *race, on the* . . . .
Her distinguishing flag is . . . .
her sail numbers and letters are . . . . . . , *her rig is* . . . . . .
the color of her hull is . . . .
and her rating or class is . . . .
   I agree to be bound by the rules of the I.Y.R.U., by the prescriptions of the national authority under which this race is sailed, by the sailing instructions and by the class rules.
   Signed . . . . *Date* . . . .
     (*Owner or owner's representative*)
       Name . . . .
       Address . . . .
       Telephone No. . . . .
       Club . . . .
Entrance fee enclosed

25—Sail Numbers, Letters, and Emblems

2. Other yachts shall comply with the rules of their national authority or class in regard to the allotment, carrying, and size of sail numbers, letters, and emblems, which rules should, so far as they may be applicable, conform to the above requirements.

28—Flags

A national authority may prescribe the flag usage which shall be observed by yachts under its jurisdiction.

72—Disqualification After Protest

4. The question of damages arising from an infringement of any of these rules or the sailing in-

structions shall be governed by the prescriptions, if any, of the national authority.

77—Appeals

1. Unless otherwise prescribed by the national authority which has recognized the sponsoring organization concerned, an appeal against the decision of a race committee shall be governed by rules 77, Appeals, and 78, Particulars to be Furnished in Appeals.

2. Unless otherwise prescribed by the national authority or in the sailing instructions (subject to rule 2(j) or 3.2(b)(xvi)), a protest which has been decided by the race committee shall be referred to the national authority solely on a question of interpretation of these rules, within such period after the receipt of the race committee's decision, as the national authority may decide:

(a) when the race committee, at its own instance, thinks proper to do so, or

(b) when any of the parties involved in the protest makes application for such reference.

This reference shall be accompanied by such deposit as the national authority may prescribe, payable by the appellant, to be forfeited to the funds of the national authority in the event of the appeal being dismissed.

3. The national authority shall have power to uphold or reverse the decision of the race committee, and if it is of opinion, from the facts found by the race committee, that a yacht involved in a protest has infringed an applicable rule, it shall disqualify her, irrespective of whether the rule or sailing instruction which led to such disqualification was mentioned in the protest.

4. The decision of the national authority, which shall be final, shall be communicated in writing to all interested parties.

5. In the Olympic Games and such other international regattas as may be specially approved by the I.Y.R.U., the decisions of the race committee, jury or judges shall be final.

6. An appeal once lodged with the national authority shall not be withdrawn.

78—Particulars to be Furnished in Appeals

1. The reference to the national authority shall be in writing and shall contain the following particulars, in order, so far as they are applicable:

(a) A copy of the notice of the race and the sailing instructions furnished to the yachts.

(b) A copy of the protest, or protests, if any, prepared in accordance with rule 68.3 (d), and all other written statements which may have been put in by the parties.

(c) The observations of the race committee thereon, a full statement of the facts found, its decision and the grounds thereof.

(d) An official diagram prepared by the race committee in accordance with the facts found by it, showing:

(i) The course to the next mark, or, if close by, the mark itself with the required side;

(ii) the direction and force of the wind;

(iii) the set and strength of the current, if any;

(iv) the depth of water, if relevant; and

(v) the positions and courses of all the yachts involved.

(vi) Where possible, yachts should be shown sailing from the bottom of the diagram towards the top.

(e) The grounds of the appeal, to be supplied by either:

(i) the race committee under rule 77.2(a); or

(ii) the appellant under rule 77.2(b).

(f) Observations, if any, upon the appeal by the race committee or any of the parties.

2. The race committee shall notify all parties that an appeal will be lodged and shall invite them to make any observations upon it. Any such observation shall be forwarded with the appeal.

APPENDIX IV

EXCERPTS FROM THE INTERNATIONAL REGULATIONS FOR PREVENTING COLLISIONS AT SEA—1963

(Commonly called the International Rules of the Road)

PART B.—LIGHTS AND SHAPES

RULE 5

(b) In addition to the lights prescribed in section (a), a sailing vessel may carry on the top of the foremast two lights in a vertical line one over the other, sufficiently separated so as to be clearly distinguished. The upper light shall be red and the lower light shall be green. Both lights shall be constructed and fixed as prescribed in rule 2(a)(i) and shall be visible at a distance of at least 2 miles.

[NOTE: 2(a)(i) calls for a light "to show an unbroken light over an arc of the horizon of 225° so fixed as to show from right ahead to 2 points abaft the beam on either side."]

Rule 12

Every vessel or seaplane on the water may, if necessary in order to attract attention, in addition to the lights which she is by these rules required to carry, show a flare up light or use a detonating or other efficient sound signal that cannot be mistaken for any signal authorized elsewhere under these rules.

PART D.—STEERING AND SAILING RULES

Preliminary

1. *In obeying and construing these rules, any action taken should be positive, in ample time, and with due regard to the observance of good seamanship.*

2. *Risk of collison can, when circumstances permit, be ascertained by carefully watching the compass bearing of an approaching vessel. If the bearing does not appreciably change, such risk should be deemed to exist.*

4. *Rules 17 to 24 apply only to vessels in sight of one another.*

Rule 17

(a) When two sailing vessels are approaching one another, so as to involve risk of collision, one of them shall keep out of the way of the other as follows:

(i) When each has the wind on a different side, the vessel which has the wind on the port side shall keep out of the way of the other.

(ii) When both have the wind on the same side, the vessel which is to windward shall keep out of the way of the vessel which is to leeward.

(b) For the purposes of this rule the windward side shall be deemed to be the side opposite to that on which the mainsail is carried or, in the case of a square-rigged vessel, the side opposite to that on which the largest fore-and-aft sail is carried.

Rule 20

(a) When a power-driven vessel and a sailing vessel are proceeding in such directions as to involve risk of collision, except as provided for in rules 24 and 26, the power-driven vessel shall keep out of the way of the sailing vessel.

(b) This rule shall not give to a sailing vessel the right to hamper, in a narrow channel, the safe passage of a power-driven vessel which can navigate only inside such channel.

Rule 22

Every vessel which is directed by these rules to keep out of the way of another vessel shall, so far as possible, take positive early action to comply with this obligation, and shall, if the circumstances of the case admit, avoid crossing ahead of the other.

Rule 24

Notwithstanding anything contained in these rules, every vessel overtaking any other shall keep out of the way of the overtaken vessel.

(b) Every vessel coming up with another vessel from any direction more than 22½° (2 points) abaft her beam, i.e., in such a position, with reference to the vessel which she is overtaking, that at night she would be unable to see either of that vessel's sidelights, shall be deemed to be an overtaking vessel; and no subsequent alteration of the bearing between the two vessels shall make the overtaking vessel a crossing vessel within the meaning of these rules, or relieve her of the duty of keeping clear of the overtaken vessel until she is finally past and clear.

(c) If the overtaking vessel cannot determine with certainty whether she is forward of or abaft this direction from the other vessel, she shall assume that she is an overtaking vessel and keep out of the way.

Rule 26

All vessels not engaged in fishing, except vessels to which the provisions of rule 4 apply, shall, when underway, keep out of the way of vessels engaged in fishing.

The International Rules apply to vessels on the high seas. The Inland Rules apply to vessels on inland waters including coastal areas.

Copies of the complete regulations, both International and Inland, may be obtained from the United States Coast Guard.

PROTEST COMMITTEE PROCEDURE
in Outline Form

Rules Concerning Protests—
68, 69, 70, 71, 72, 73 and 75.

Preliminaries

1. Note on the protest the time it is received.
2. Determine whether the protest contains the information called for by rule 68.3(d) in sufficient detail to identify the incident and to tell the recipient what the protest is about. If not, ask the protestor to supply the information (rule 68.3(f)).
3. Inquire whether the protestor flew a protest flag in accordance with rule 68.3(a) unless

rule 68.3(b) applies or the protestor is seeking redress under rule 68.5(a) and note his answer on the protest.
4. Inquire whether the protestor tried to inform the yacht(s) protested against (the protestee(s)) that a protest would be lodged (rule 68.3(c)) and note his answer on the protest.
5. Unless rule 69 applies, promptly notify the protestee(s).
6. Hold a hearing as soon as possible when the protest conforms to the requirements of rule 68 (see 1, 2 and 3 above). Notify the representative of each yacht involved of the time and place of the hearing (rule 70.1).

The Hearing

1. The representative of each yacht involved in the incident is entitled to be present throughout the hearing. All others, except one witness at a time while testifying, may be excluded (rule 70.1).
2. Read to the meeting the protest and any other written statement there may be about the incident (such as an account of it from the protestee).
3. Have first the protestor and then the protestee(s) give their accounts of the incident. Each may question the other(s). Questions by the protest committee, except for clarifying details, are preferably deferred until all accounts have been presented. Models are helpful. Positions before and after the incident itself are often helpful.
4. Invite the protestor and then the protestee to call witnesses. They may be questioned by the protestor and protestees as well as by the committee.
5. Invite first the protestor and then the protestee to make a final statement of his case, including any application or interpretation of the rules to the incident as he sees it.

Decision

1. The protest committee, after dismissing those involved in the incident, should decide what the relevant facts are.

2. The committee should then apply the rules and reach a decision as to who, if anyone, infringed a rule and what rule was infringed (rule 71).

3. Having reached a decision, it should record both the findings of fact and the decision in writing, recall the protestor and protestee and read to them the decision (rule 71).

4. Any party involved is entitled to a copy of the decision (rule 71), signed by the chairman of the protest committee. A copy should also be filed with the committee records.

N.B. The protest committee referred to above may be the race committee judges appointed for the event in which the incident occurred or a protest committee established by the race committee for the express purpose of handling protests.

Standard Protest Forms are available from the N.A.Y.R.U. at $1.25 for sets of 25.

APPLICATION FOR MEMBERSHIP

NAME (*in block letters*) ....

ADDRESS ....

.... Zip Code .....

YACHT CLUB ....

YACHT (if any) ....

Check   Sustaining Membership   ($25.)
   for annual dues
Money Order   Contributing Membership   ($15.)
enclosed herewith.   Regular Membership   ($10.)*
                       Yacht Club Membership   ($15.)

Please mail the Year Book, Bulletins and any other data to the address shown above.

* Persons under 25 years of age   ($5.)

Please return this form to the

North American Yacht Racing Union
37 West 44th Street
New York, N.Y. 10036

PUBLICATIONS

1969 NAYRU Racing and Team Racing Rules as adopted from the IYRU Rules.

Time Allowance Tables:
Table 1 with allowances in seconds per mile and
Table 3 with allowances in decimal hours, both for tenths of a foot in rating, are combined;
Table 2 with allowances in seconds per mile and
Table 4 with allowances in decimal hours, both for hundredths of a foot of rating, are combined.

Offshore Racing Recommended Minimum Equipment Lists.

Decisions on Appeals from the Racing Rules.

Leatherette, gold-stamped binder for Decisions on Appeals and supplements thereto.

International Case Law (Appeals Decisions published by the IYRU omitting reprints of NAYRU Decisions).

Race Committee Handbook—an illustrated manual covering all aspects of planning and conducting regattas including protest hearing procedures.

Protest Forms (required by many associations and clubs).

Cruising Club of America Measurement Rule.

International Code Flags and Pennants in color.

Yacht Race Scoring by F. Gregg Bemis (available only from John DeGraff, Inc., 34 Oak Ave., Tuckahoe, N.Y. 10707—$3.75).

NAYRU LAPEL BUTTON—gold plated and enamelled.

NAYRU NECKTIE—blue with miniaturized lighthouse in red.

RACE COMMITTEE SIGNALS

See Rule 4. (*See also next page for pennants.*)

AP—Answering Pennant Postponement Signal

L—Come Within Hail or Follow Me

M—Mark Signal

N—Abandonment Signal

N over X—Abandonment and Resail Signal

N over 1st Repeater—Cancellation Signal

R—Reverse Course Signal

S—Shortened Course Signal

1st Repeater—General Recall Signal

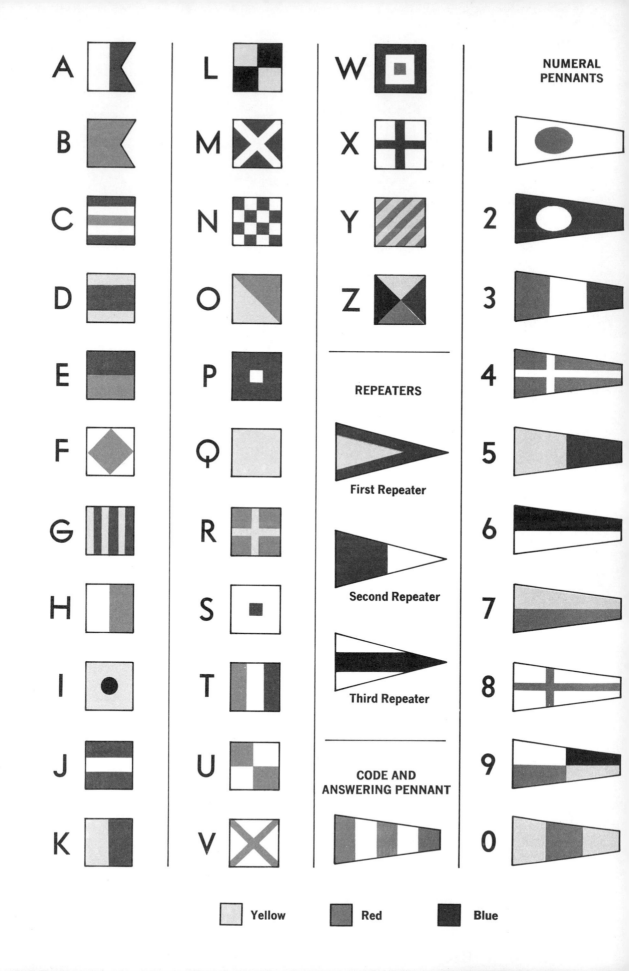

NUMERAL PENNANTS

REPEATERS

First Repeater

Second Repeater

Third Repeater

CODE AND ANSWERING PENNANT

Yellow   Red   Blue

Glossary of Sailing Terms

Glossary of Sailing Terms

Abaft, toward the stern.

Abaft the beam, any direction between the beam and the stern.

Abandonment, an abandoned race is one that the race committee declares void at any time after the starting signal, and that can be resailed at its discretion.

Abeam, the direction at right angles to the centerline of the boat.

About ship, the order to tack ship.

Abreast, opposite or at right angles to.

Adrift, not being fast to a stationary object.

Aft, toward the stern.

Aground, on the bottom.

Alee, away from the direction of the wind, referring to the helm or tiller.

Aloft, above the deck; overhead.

Amidships, on the line of the keel, midway between bow and stern.

Anchor light, a white light visible all around the horizon, displayed from the forward part of a vessel at anchor.

Anchorage, a suitable place for anchoring.

Astern, backward; somewhere behind.

Athwart or athwartships, at right angles to the centerline.

Auxiliary, a yacht propelled by both sail and power.

Back, the wind backs when its direction changes counterclockwise.

Backstays, standing rigging that supports the mast from aft.

Backwind, wind that is deflected from its normal course by a yacht's sails.

Balloon jib, a large headsail with considerable draft, generally used in light weather.

Bare poles, a yacht under way with no sails set.

Barge, in racing, to force one's way—against the rules—between another yacht and a starting mark.

Battens, light, thin strips of wood inserted in pockets in the sail to extend the leach.

Beam, the greatest width of a vessel. See Abeam.

Beam wind, one which blows athwart a vessel's fore-and-aft line.

Bear, to bear down is to approach from windward. To bear off is to up-helm and run more to leeward.

Bearing, the direction of an object expressed in terms of compass points or degrees.

Beating, working to windward by a succession of tacks.

Beaufort Scale, a table used for describing the velocity of the wind.

Becket, an eye in the end of a block to which a rope may be secured.

Before the wind, having the wind coming from aft.

Belay, to make fast a rope or line.

Bend, to fasten one rope end to another.

Bight, any segment of a rope between the ends.

Bilge, the turn of the hull below the waterline.

Bitt, a vertical post extending above the deck to which mooring lines are made fast.

Blanket, to take the wind from the sails of a yacht that is to leeward of you.

Block, a device consisting of a frame or shell which contains a sheave over which a rope is run. Blocks with a rope through them form a tackle.

Board, a leg or tack when close-hauled. It might be a long board or a short board.

Bolt rope, a rope sewed to the edges of a sail to give it strength.

Boom, generally, a spar at the foot of a fore-and-aft sail.

Boom vang, a tackle secured to the boom to prevent it from lifting on a reach or run and to flatten the sail.

Boot-topping, a painted stripe along the waterline, separating the topside from the bottom paint.

Bow, the forward part of a vessel.

Bowline, a knot used to form an eye or loop in the end of a rope.

Bowsprit, a spar extending forward of the bow, to support the headsails.

Brightwork, all wood members that are varnished.

Bristol fashion, kept in a seaman-like style.

Broach to, to swing around toward the wind in a dangerous manner when running free because of bad steering or the forces of heavy wind and sea. A frequent cause of capsizing.

Bunt, when furling, the middle part of a sail.

Burdened vessel, the one which must keep clear of those having right of way.

Bury, that part of a mast which is below the deck.

By the wind, sailing close-hauled.

Cable, the rope or chain that is secured to the anchor.

Cancellation, a cancelled race is one that the race committee decides will not be sailed thereafter.

Capsize, to turn over.

Cast off, to let go a line.

Cat boat, a craft with a mast stepped far forward, carrying a single sail.

Catamaran, a craft with two hulls joined by crossbeams.

Catenary, the curve of a rope suspended between two points, such as the anchor rode or towing line.

Center of effort, the center of wind pressure on the sail area.

Centerboard, a flat board or member that is raised and lowered in a watertight box called the trunk or well. Its purpose is to add keel area to a shoal draft boat and to reduce leeway.

Chafing gear, canvas or other material secured about a rope or cable to protect it from wear and abrasion.

Chain plates, metal straps bolted to the sides of a yacht, to which the shrouds are attached.

Cheek block, a block whose sheave is mounted against the side of a spar.

Chine, the line of intersection between the sides and bottom of a flat- or V-bottomed boat.

Clear, free, not entangled.

Clear astern and clear ahead, a yacht is clear astern of another when her hull and equip-

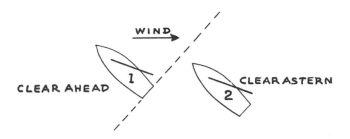

ment are abaft an imaginary line projected abeam from the aftermost point of the other's hull and equipment. The other yacht is clear ahead.

Clear for running, a sheet or halyard coiled down so that it will run out quickly without becoming tangled.

Cleat, a device of wood or metal with two horns around which ropes are made fast.

Clew, the lower, after corner of a fore-and-aft sail.

Clew outhaul, the tackle by which the clew is hauled out on the boom.

Clinker-built, a method of planking in which the lower edge of a plank overlaps the upper edge of the one below it. Also called lapstrake.

Close aboard, in close proximity to.

Close-hauled, sailing as close to the wind as possible.

Close-winded, a yacht capable of sailing very close to the wind.

Clove hitch, a method of making a line fast to a spar or rope.

Coil, to lay a rope down in circular turns. Rope is sold by the coil, which contains 200 fathoms.

Colors, the ceremony of hoisting the national flag at 8 A.M. The lowering at sunset is called making colors.

Compass course, the direction of a ship's heading based on the ship's compass.

Compass error, the amount the compass is deflected from the true direction by variation and deviation combined.

Compass rose, a circle graduated in points, or degrees, or both, from which courses can be taken.

Counter, the underside of the overhang of the after part of the hull.

Course, the direction steered by a vessel.

Course protractor, an instrument having a compass rose and a movable arm by which courses may be laid down on a chart or bearings noted.

Cringle, a circular eye of rope around a thimble, worked in the leach and clew of a sail; as the reef cringle and the clew cringle.

Cross bearing, two or more bearings of as many known objects are noted and plotted on the chart, in order to determine the ship's position. This will be at the point of intersection of these bearings.

Cuddy, a diminutive cabin in a small boat.

Current, the horizontal movement of water. Currents may be periodic, due to the effect of the tides, or seasonal, due to seasonal winds.

Dagger board, a type of centerboard which does not pivot on a hinge but is raised and lowered vertically in the trunk.

Deviation, the errors of the compass due to the effect of local magnetic attraction.

Deviation card, a tabulation of the vessel's heading on each point of the compass and the deviation which appears when steering on each.

Dinghy, a small rowboat.

Dink, nickname for dinghy.

Displacement, the weight of the water displaced by a floating vessel, which is equal to the weight of the vessel.

Ditty bag, receptacle for a sailor's sewing kit.

Douse, to take in a sail quickly.

Downhaul boom, tackle attached to the gooseneck, by which the boom is pulled down after the sail is hoisted, to tighten the luff.

Down helm and up helm, down is away from, and up is toward the wind. The helm is put down to tack or luff, and up to jibe or bear away.

Downwind, to leeward.

Draft, the depth of water necessary to float a vessel.

Drift, a vessel's leeway.

Ease her, to luff a bit in heavy weather.

Ebb, the period when the tidal current is flowing away from the land.

Eye splice, a loop spliced into the end of a rope.

Fair wind, the wind abaft the beam.

Falling off, paying off away from the wind.

Fast, to make fast is to secure.

Fathom, a measure of depth equaling six feet.

Feathering, alternately bearing off and pointing higher than the normal close-hauled angle to the wind, generally employed in puffy winds.

Fetch, a yacht fetches when, sailing close-hauled, it arrives at or to windward of a given object or point.

Figure-eight knot, a knot made in the end of a rope to prevent its unreeving through a block.

Finishing, a yacht finishes when any part of her hull, crew, or equipment, in normal position, crosses the finishing line from the direction of the last mark.

Fisherman's bend, a method of making the cable fast to the anchor.

Fix, a vessel's position located on the chart by two or more bearings on known landmarks.

Flake, a complete round turn in coiling down a rope.

Flatten in, to trim in the sheets.

Flaw, a gust of wind heavier than the prevailing breeze.

Flood, the period when the tidal current is flowing toward the land.

Fly, a small wind pennant at the masthead.

Foot, the lower edge of a sail. To make maximum speed through the water when beating to windward.

Fore and aft, in line with the keel.

Forefoot, the point at which the stem joins the keel.

Forepeak, the compartment or space in the very forward part of a vessel.

Fore reach, the headway a vessel makes when luffed into the wind.

Foresail, in a schooner, the sail set from the foremast.

Forestay, a stay ahead of the jibstay, leading to the masthead.

Forward, toward the bow.

Forward of the beam, any direction less than 90 degrees from the bow.

Foul, the opposite of clear. In racing, a breaking of the rules.

Found, furnished. A vessel is well found if she is well equipped.

Free, to sail with the wind aft, but in racing, a yacht is sailing free when not sailing close-hauled.

Freeboard, the distance from the edge of the deck to the water.

Full and by, when all sails are full and drawing, and the course is as close to the wind as possible.

Gaff, a spar that supports the head of a fore-and-aft sail.

Garboard, the plank or strake next to the keel.

Gasket, a sail stop.

Ghosting, a yacht making headway when there is no apparent wind.

Gilguy, a lanyard used to tie off a halyard to prevent it from slatting against the mast.

Go about, to tack.

Go adrift, to break loose.

Gooseneck, the fitting which secures the boom to the mast.

Ground, to touch bottom.

Ground swell, long undulations seen during calm or light airs, due to waves running into shoaling water.

Ground tackle, the anchor and its cable and/or chain.

Gunwale (Gunnel), the rail of a boat.

Half hitch, a turn made around a rope or spar with the end coming through the bight.

Halyards, ropes for hoisting sails.

Hard-a-lee, the tiller put hard over, away from the wind. The command given preparatory to coming about.

Head, the upper corner of a sail. Also the toilet compartment.

Head sails, the sails forward of the mast.

Head up, to luff.

Header, a sudden wind shift toward the bow.

Helm, the tiller.

Hitch, a combination of turns for making a rope fast to a spar or another rope.

Hogged, a term applied to an aged vessel whose bow and stern have drooped.

In stays, losing all headway, with sails luffing, midway in the act of going about.

In irons, same as "in stays."

Irish pennant, a loose end hanging about the sails or rigging.

Jib, a triangular sail set ahead of the mast on the jibstay.

Jibing, a yacht begins to jibe at the moment when, with the wind aft, the foot of her mainsail crosses her centerline; she completes the jibe when the mainsail has filled on the other tack.

Knockdown, thrown on her beam-ends by a sudden gust or squall.

Knot, a measure of speed, meaning velocity in nautical miles per hour.

Land breeze, an evening wind coming off the land.

Lanyard, a short line used for making anything fast.

Lay (verb), a yacht lays her course if when

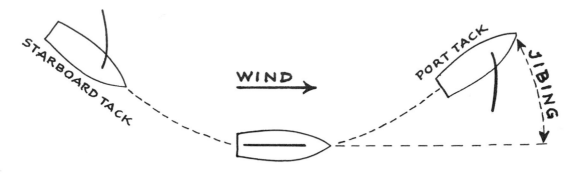

Jumper stay, a trusslike stay on the upper forward side of the mast.

Kedge, a light anchor used for kedging off.

Kedging off, freeing a vessel that is aground by heaving in a cable fast to an anchor that has been carried out into deep water by a dinghy.

Keep her full, the order to keep the sails drawing.

Ketch, a two-masted yacht in which the smaller, after mast is stepped forward of the rudder post.

close-hauled she is able to fetch her objective point.

Lay (noun), the twist of a rope's strands. If twisted to the right, it is right laid.

Lazarette, a stowage compartment in the stern.

Leach, the after edge of a sail.

Lee bowing the tide, sailing with the current setting against the lee bow, thus pushing the bow toward the wind.

Lee helm, carrying the tiller pushed to leeward to keep the vessel on course. Not as desirable as weather helm.

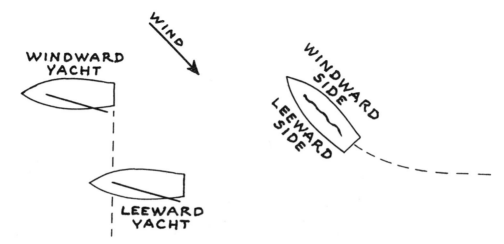

Leeward and windward, the leeward side of a yacht is that on which she is carrying her mainsail or, if luffing head to wind, *was* carrying her mainsail. The opposite side is the windward side. When neither of two yachts on the same tack is clear astern, the one on the leeward side of the other is the leeward yacht. The other is the windward yacht.

Leeway, the amount a vessel is carried to leeward by the force of the wind.

Leg, a tack. The course from one mark to another.

Lift, a sudden wind shift away from the bow.

Light sails, the spinnaker, balloon jib, and mizzen staysail.

Limbers, holes in the frames next to the keel to allow bilge water to drain to the lowest part.

Lines, ropes used for various purposes, such as clew lines or dock lines.

Locker, a closet or small stowage compartment.

Log book, a record of all activities aboard a vessel.

Long splice, joining the ends of two ropes in such a manner that the splice will pass freely through a block.

Loose-footed, a sail without a boom, or secured to a boom at the tack and clew only.

Lubber line, a line on the forward inner side of the compass bowl, which represents the bow of the ship and is used to steer a course.

Luff, to alter course more nearly into the wind. The forward edge of a sail.

Magnetic bearing, the direction of an object, with no deviation.

Magnetic course, the ship's heading based on the magnetic compass.

Mainmast, the forward mast of a yawl or ketch.

Mark, a mark is any object, specified in the sailing instructions, that a yacht must round or pass on a required side.

Marline, two-stranded twine of tarred hemp.

Marlinspike, a pointed steel tool for opening rope strands when splicing.

Marlinspike sailor, one who is adept at splicing, knotting, and manipulation of rope and canvas.

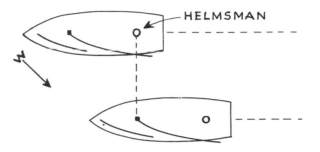

Mast abeam, when a leeward yacht overlaps a windward yacht to a point where the mast of the leeward yacht is directly abeam of the windward yacht's helmsman at his normal station, the position of mast abeam has occurred. The point is sighted at 90 degrees from the centerline of the windward yacht's helmsman to determine the mast abeam position.

Mast coat, a canvas sleeve or boot around the mast at the deck, to prevent the entry of water.

Mast step, the timber on which the mast rests.

Mile, the nautical or sea mile is 6080 feet.

Miss stays, to fail in the attempt to go about.

Mizzen, the after sail of a ketch or yawl.

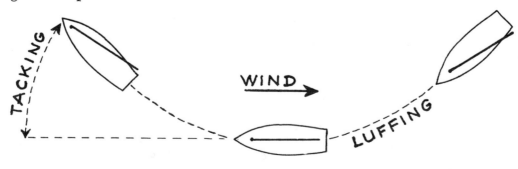

Moorings, heavy anchors and chains permanently in position.

Nun, a truncated conical buoy painted red and bearing an even number, marking the starboard side of a channel entering port.

Obstruction, an obstruction is any object, including craft under way, large enough to require a yacht, if not less than one overall length away from it, to make a substantial alteration of course to pass on one side or the other, or any object that can be passed on one side only, including a buoy, when the yacht in question cannot safely pass between it and the shoal or object that it marks.

Off soundings, at sea, beyond the 100-fathom curve.

Off the wind, to sail with the sheets slacked off.

Offing, in sight of land, but well to seaward.

Offshore wind, one blowing off the land.

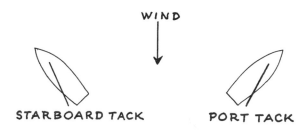

On a tack, a yacht is on a tack except when she is going through the act of tacking or jibing. A yacht is on the tack (starboard or port) corresponding to her windward side.

On the wind, close-hauled.

Outhaul, a line used to haul the corner of a sail out to the end of the boom or gaff.

Outpoint, to sail closer to the wind than another vessel.

Overlap, two yachts overlap if neither is clear astern; or if, although one is clear astern, an intervening yacht overlaps both of them. The terms clear astern, clear ahead, and overlap apply to yachts on opposite tacks only when they are subject to rule 42—Rounding or Passing Marks and Obstructions.

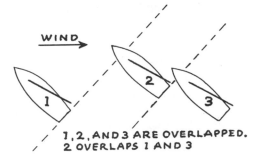

Painter, the rope secured to the bow of a dinghy for towing or making fast.

Palm, a sailor's thimble. It is of leather and fits over the hand.

Parallel rulers, an instrument used in chart work for transferring courses and bearings to and from the compass rose.

Pay off, to swing away from the wind.

Pay out, to ease out a rope.

Pinching her, sailing too close to the wind.

Point, the ability to sail close to the wind. "She points well."

Port, the left side of a vessel, looking forward.

Port tack, sailing with the wind coming over the port side.

Postponement, a postponed race is one that is not started at its scheduled time and that can be sailed at any time the race committee may decide.

Pram, a dinghy having square ends.

Privileged vessel, the one having the right of way.

Proper course, a proper course is any course that a yacht might sail after the starting signal, in the absence of the other yacht or yachts affected, to finish as quickly as possible. The course sailed before luffing or bearing away is presumably, but not necessarily, the yacht's proper course. There is no proper course before the starting signal.

Purchase, a tackle.

Quarter, the part of a yacht forward of the stern and aft of the shrouds; off the quarter is in a direction 45 degrees from dead astern.

Racing, a yacht is racing from her preparatory signal until she has either finished and cleared the finishing line and finishing marks or has retired, or until the race has been cancelled, postponed, or abandoned, except that, in match or team races, the sailing instructions may prescribe that a yacht is racing from any specified time before the preparatory signal.

Rake, the angle the mast makes with the perpendicular.

Range, two objects in line to indicate a course to be steered.

Rap full, a little off the wind, with all sails drawing well.

Reach, a long tack with the wind abeam or a little forward or aft of abeam.

Ready about, the order to tack.

Reef, to reduce sail area.

Reef points, short pieces of line set in a sail for reefing purposes.

Reeve, to pass a rope through a block.

Right of way, the right to hold one's course.

Roach, the curve in the leach of a sail.

Rode, the anchor line or cable.

Rolling hitch, one used on a spar where a knot is needed for a lengthwise pull.

Round turn, to pass a line completely around a cleat, spar, or another rope.

Rules of the road, laws of navigation designed to avoid collision. They include steering, lights, and fog or whistle signals.

Runners, backstays which can be set up or slacked off while under way.

Running, sailing with the wind astern.

Running rigging, all lines used to control the sails.

Sag off, to make excessive leeway.

Sea lawyer, an argumentative sailor.

Sea room, a good safe distance from shoals or the shore.

Seize, to bind with marline or small stuff.

Set, the direction in which a current flows.

Sharpen up, to come more into the wind.

Sheave, the roller in a block.

Sheer, the upward curve of the deck, viewed from the side.

Sheet, the rope used to trim a sail.

Sheet bend, a handy knot for joining two rope's ends.

Short splice, to permanently join two pieces of rope. It will not pass through a block since it increases the diameter.

Shrouds, rigging which stays a mast at the sides.

Slack away, to pay out.

Slack water, the period between flood and ebb tides when no current exists.

Slant, a favorable wind.

Sloop, a one-masted vessel carrying a mainsail and jib.

Snatch block, one having an opening in the side into which a bight of a rope can be placed, without hauling the whole length through.

Snub, to check the running out of a rope or line by taking a turn around a cleat or bitt.

Spars, a term applied to all booms, gaffs, masts, etc.

Spinnaker, a light, spherical sail used in reaching and running.

Splice, to join two ropes by tucking their strands over and under each other in various manners.

Split tacks, to take the opposite tack when sailing to windward with another yacht.

Spring line, a dock line leading forward or aft to prevent a vessel from moving ahead or astern.

Square knot, a knot consisting of two overhand knots used for tying reef points.

Standing part, the part of a rope that is made fast.

Standing rigging, the shrouds and stays that support the mast.

Starboard, the right side of a vessel, looking forward.

Starboard tack, sailing with the wind coming over the starboard side.

Starting, a yacht starts when, after her starting signal, any part of her hull, crew, or equipment first crosses the starting line in the direction of the first mark.

Stays, rigging supporting the mast from forward or aft.

Staysail, a triangular fore-and-aft sail set from various stays.

Steerageway, sufficient headway for the rudder to act.

Stern, the afterpart of a vessel.

Stops, pieces of line or canvas strips used to secure a sail when furling it.

Tabernacle, a sort of hinge in the mast, near the deck, by which it may be lowered.

Tack, the lower forward corner of a sail.

Tacking, a yacht is tacking from the moment she is beyond head to wind until she has borne away, if beating to windward, to a close-hauled course; if not beating to windward, to the course on which her mainsail has filled.

Tackle, a purchase composed of blocks and rope.

Tang, a metal strap secured to the mast to which a shroud, stay, or halyard block is secured.

Telltale, a bit of ribbon or yarn tied on the shrouds to indicate direction of apparent wind.

Tender, a vessel that lacks stability.

Thwarts, seats in a small boat.

Thwartships, crosswise of the deck, from side to side.

Tide rips, patches of very disturbed or broken water caused by strong tidal currents.

Tiller, the member attached to the head of the rudder, by means of which the boat is steered.

Topping lift, a line or tackle from the masthead supporting the boom at its after end.

Traveler, a track secured to the deck carrying a movable block, by means of which the lead of a sheet may be changed as desired.

True course, a course steered by a ship's compass that has been corrected for variation and deviation.

Unbend, to cast adrift.

Unmoor, to heave up the anchor or cast off mooring or dock lines.

Unreeve, to haul a rope completely out of a block.

Unship, to detach or remove anything from its proper place.

Up helm, see "down helm."

Vang, see "boom vang."

Variation, the difference in degrees between magnetic north and true north.

Veer, when the wind changes direction to the right, it is said to veer.

Wake, the track a vessel leaves astern.

Way, a vessel's movement through the water.

Weather, the side from which the wind is blowing.

Weather helm, the tendency of a vessel to come up into the wind.

Whipping, winding twice about the end of a rope to keep it from unlaying.

Wind shadow, the path of dead air in the lee of a yacht.

Wind's eye, the true wind direction.

Yawl, a two-masted yacht in which the smaller, aftermast is stepped abaft the rudder post.

Index

INDEX